maranGraphics'™
Simplified User Guide for
LOTUS® *1-2-3*® *for Windows*™

Richard Maran and
Ruth Maran

maranGraphics Inc.
Mississauga, Ontario, Canada

Distributed in United States
by Regents/Prentice Hall

Telephone:	1-800-223-1360
Fax:	1-800-445-6991

Distributed in Canada
by Prentice Hall Canada

Telephone:	1-800-567-3800
Fax:	416-299-2529

Distributed Internationally
by Simon & Schuster

Telephone:	201-767-4900
Fax:	201-767-5625

maranGraphics' ™ Simplified User Guide for
LOTUS® 1-2-3® for Windows™

Acknowledgements

Library of Congress Cataloging-in-Publication Data

Maran, Richard
     MaranGraphics simplified user guide for Lotus 1-2-3
for Windows/Richard Maran and Ruth Maran.
          p.   cm.
Includes index.
ISBN 0-13-000779-X

     1. Lotus 1-2-3 (Computer file). 2. Business--Computer
programs. 3. Electronic spreadsheets. 4. Business--
Graphic methods--Computer programs. I. Maran, Ruth,
1970-   . II.Title. III. Title: Lotus 1-2-3 for Windows.

HF5548.4.L67M3243   1993
650'.0285'5369--dc20   92-42754
                                                      CIP

Special thanks to Mr. Charles (Chuck) E. Tatham
of Lotus Development Canada Ltd., and
Mr. Saverio C. Tropiano for their support and
consultation.

To the dedicated staff at maranGraphics Inc.
and HyperImage Inc., including Monica DeVries,
Lynne Hoppen, Jim C. Leung, Robert Maran,
Elizabeth Seeto, and Branimir Zlamalik for their
artistic contribution.

To Eric Feistmantl who was always there to solve
our technical and operational problems.

And finally to Maxine Maran for providing the
organizational skill to keep the project under
control.

Cover Design:
Erich Volk

Production:
Monica DeVries
Jim C. Leung
Branimir Zlamalik

Linotronic L-300 Output:
HyperImage Inc.

Table of Contents

This Simplified User Guide displays –on each page– exactly what you see on the screen as you move through Lotus® 1-2-3® for Windows.

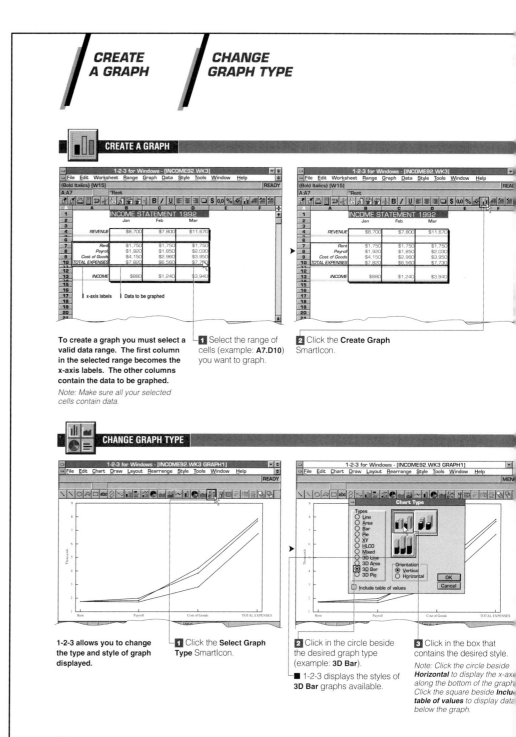

CREATE A GRAPH

CHANGE GRAPH TYPE

CREATE A GRAPH

To create a graph you must select a valid data range. The first column in the selected range becomes the x-axis labels. The other columns contain the data to be graphed.

Note: Make sure all your selected cells contain data.

1 Select the range of cells (example: **A7.D10**) you want to graph.

2 Click the **Create Graph** SmartIcon.

CHANGE GRAPH TYPE

1-2-3 allows you to change the type and style of graph displayed.

1 Click the **Select Graph Type** SmartIcon.

2 Click in the circle beside the desired graph type (example: **3D Bar**).

■ 1-2-3 displays the styles of **3D Bar** graphs available.

3 Click in the box that contains the desired style.

Note: Click the circle beside Horizontal to display the x-axis along the bottom of the graph. Click the square beside Include table of values to display data below the graph.

70 ▶

2 ▶

USING
THIS GUIDE

START
1-2-3

OPEN A NEW
WORKSHEET FILE

MAXIMIZE
AND RESTORE
A WINDOW

SWITCH
BETWEEN
WINDOWS

HELP

CLOSE
WINDOWS

EXIT
1 2-3

GETTING
STARTED

■ All topics within the current chapter are displayed. The current topic is highlighted in red type.

MANAGE
FILES

SMARTICONS

ENTER DATA

TE
PH

CHANGE
GRAPH TYPE

ADD
A HEADING

ADD
A LEGEND

ADD GRAPH
TO WORKSHEET

RESIZE
A GRAPH

VIEW GRAPH

ADD TEXT

DRAW
OBJECTS

MOVE
AN OBJECT

DELETE
AN OBJECT

■ All chapters in the guide are displayed. The current chapter is highlighted in red type.

SAVE
AND OPEN
WORKSHEETS

MOVE
AND COPY
DATA

ROWS AND
COLUMNS

The graph is linked to the data. This means that if you later make changes to the worksheet data, the graph automatically mirrors those changes.

CHANGE
APPEARANCE
OF DATA

MULTIPLE
WORKSHEET
FILE

■ A graph is created for the selected data range (example: **A7.D10**).

Note: The first graph you create is named **GRAPH1**. The next graph created is named **GRAPH2**. The number in the graph name increases by one for each new graph created.

GETTING
STARTED

SMARTICONS

ENTER DATA

SAVE
AND OPEN
WORKSHEETS

MOVE
AND COPY
DATA

ROWS AND
COLUMNS

CHANGE
APPEARANCE
OF DATA

MULTIPLE
WORKSHEETS
FILE

CREATE
A GRAPH

PRINT

CREATE A
DATABASE

CREATE
A GRAPH

PRINT

CREATE A
DATABASE

CHANGE GRAPH TYPE
USING THE SMARTICONS

Click one of the above SmartIcons to instantly change the graph type.

4 Press **Enter** and the graph type is changed.

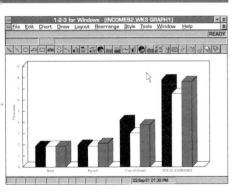

START
1-2-3

START 1-2-3 FOR WINDOWS

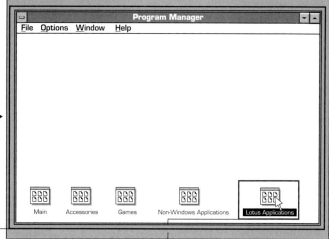

1 To start Microsoft®
Windows™ from MS-DOS,
type **win** and press **Enter**.

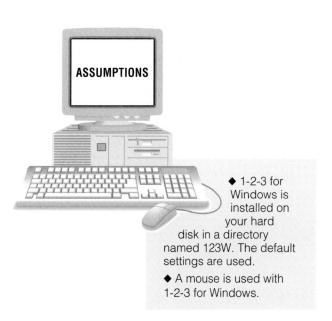

ASSUMPTIONS

◆ 1-2-3 for
Windows is
installed on
your hard
disk in a directory
named 123W. The default
settings are used.

◆ A mouse is used with
1-2-3 for Windows.

■ The **Program Manager**
window is displayed.

All your applications (example:
WordPerfect for Windows,
Lotus 1-2-3 for Windows) are
started from the Program
Manager.

The Program Manager
window contains icons which
represent group applications.
Each group icon can be
opened into a window to
display its related applications
or programs (example: the
Games group icon contains all
the Games programs).

This permits you to organize
your applications into groups
making them easier to find
and manage.

2 Move the mouse over the
group icon called **Lotus
Applications**. Click the left
button twice in quick
succession.

CONVENTIONS

If key names are separated
by a plus (+), press and hold
down the first key before
pressing the second key
(example: **Shift+Tab**).

If key names are separated
by a space press and
release the first key before
pressing the second key
(example: **Alt F**).

4 ▶

GETTING STARTED

SMARTICONS

ENTER DATA

SAVE AND OPEN WORKSHEETS

MOVE AND COPY DATA

ROWS AND COLUMNS

CHANGE APPEARANCE OF DATA

MULTIPLE WORKSHEET FILE

CREATE A GRAPH

PRINT

CREATE A DATABASE

■ The **Lotus Applications** window opens.

3 To start the **1-2-3 for Windows** application, move the mouse over its icon and click the left button twice in quick succession.

■ **1-2-3 for Windows** opens up a new worksheet file.

■ To use the numeric keypad's arrows (PgUp, PgDn, Home and End keys), the **NUM** on the Status bar must be **off**.

If **NUM** on the Status bar is **on**, press [Num Lock] to turn it **off**.

MULTIPLE WORKSHEET FILE

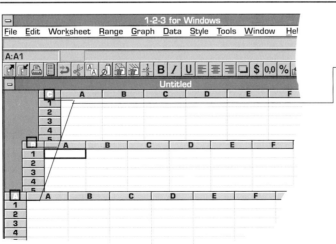

■ Each worksheet file can contain up to 256 individual worksheets.

■ Each worksheet is identified by a letter from **A** (the first worksheet), **B** (the second worksheet) to **IV** (the last worksheet).

Refer to page 64 for a full description of a Multiple Worksheet File.

OPEN A NEW
WORKSHEET FILE

OPEN A NEW WORKSHEET FILE

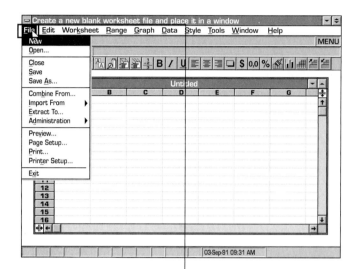

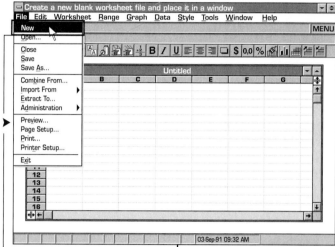

You can create new
worksheet files during a
work session, but you
can only work on one
worksheet at a time.

The first file you open is
named FILE0001.WK3.
The next file opened is
named FILE0002.WK3.
The number in the file
name increases by one
for each new file opened.

*Note: To change the name
of a worksheet file, refer to
page 34.*

1 Move the mouse ⬚ over
File and click the left button.
The **File** menu appears.

2 Move the mouse ⬚
over **New** and click the
left button.

Shortcut for Steps 1 and 2

Press **Alt F N**

TO CANCEL A MENU

Move the mouse ⬚
outside the Menu area
and click the left button.

or

Press **Esc** once or twice.

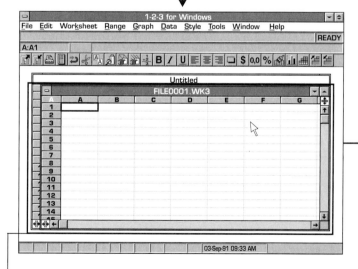

■ A new worksheet named
FILE0001.WK3 appears.

*Note: If you have previously
worked on 1-2-3, higher file
numbers may appear
(example: FILE0002.WK3 or
FILE0003.WK3).*

USING
THIS GUIDE

START
1-2-3

**OPEN A NEW
WORKSHEET FILE**

MAXIMIZE
AND RESTORE
A WINDOW

SWITCH
BETWEEN
WINDOWS

HELP

CLOSE
A WINDOW

EXIT
1-2-3

GETTING
STARTED

SMARTICONS

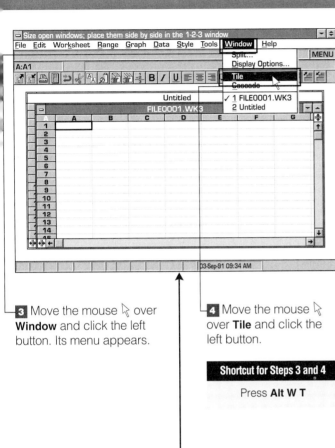

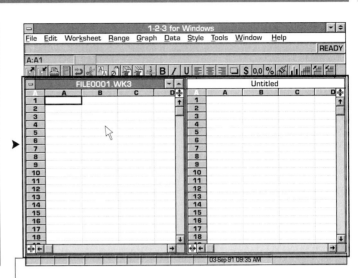

ENTER DATA

SAVE
AND OPEN
WORKSHEETS

MOVE
AND COPY
DATA

ROWS AND
COLUMNS

CHANGE
APPEARANCE
OF DATA

MULTIPLE
WORKSHEET
FILE

CREATE
A GRAPH

PRINT

CREATE A
DATABASE

3 Move the mouse � over **Window** and click the left button. Its menu appears.

4 Move the mouse � over **Tile** and click the left button.

■ **FILE0001.WK3** and **Untitled** are tiled on the workspace.

Shortcut for Steps 3 and 4

Press **Alt W T**

USING THE KEYBOARD SHORTCUT

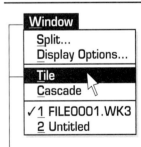

■ To select a menu command (example: **Tile**), press **Alt W T**.

W is the underlined letter for the **W**indow menu, and **T** is the underlined letter for the **T**ile command.

Note: 1-2-3 commands are not case sensitive. You can press **Alt W T** *or* **Alt w t**.

Note: If a dimmed command appears, this means it is not currently operational.

MAXIMIZE AND RESTORE A WINDOW   SWITCH BETWEEN WINDOWS

MAXIMIZE AND RESTORE A WINDOW

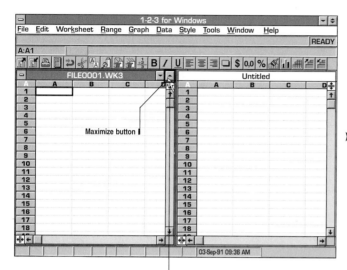

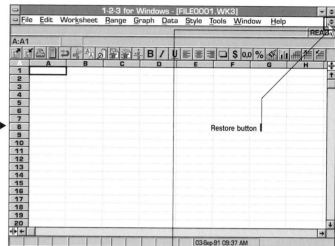

When working in a window, it can be enlarged to create a larger working area.

1 Move the mouse ⇗ over the **FILE0001.WK3** window's **Maximize** button, and click the left mouse button.

■ The **FILE0001.WK3** window is enlarged to fill the entire workspace.

2 Move the mouse ⇗ over the **FILE0001.WK3 Restore** button, and click the left mouse button.

SWITCH BETWEEN WINDOWS

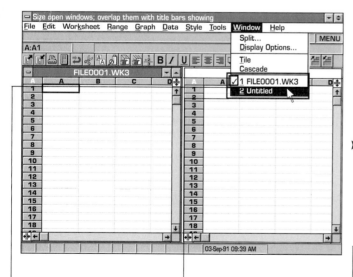

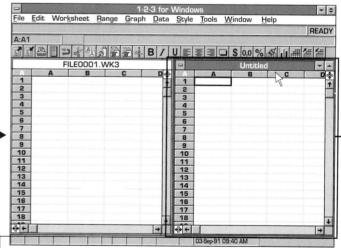

1 Press **Alt W** and the **Window** menu appears. The (✓) in front of **FILE0001.WK3** indicates its window is current.

2 To switch to another window (make it the current window), click its name in the menu (example: **Untitled**).

■ The **Untitled** window becomes the current window.

Note: This feature is useful when the window you want is completely covered by another window.

Shortcut

Click anywhere in a window to make its window current.

GETTING STARTED

SMARTICONS

ENTER DATA

SAVE AND OPEN WORKSHEETS

MOVE AND COPY DATA

ROWS AND COLUMNS

CHANGE APPEARANCE OF DATA

MULTIPLE WORKSHEET FILE

CREATE A GRAPH

PRINT

CREATE A DATABASE

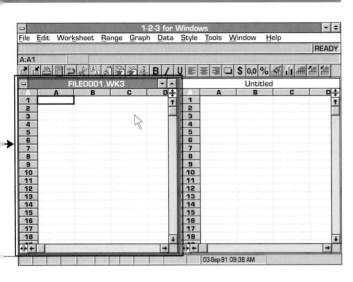

■ The **FILE0001.WK3** window is restored to its previous tiled size.

*Note: The **Untitled** window can be enlarged to occupy the complete workspace and then be restored in the same way.*

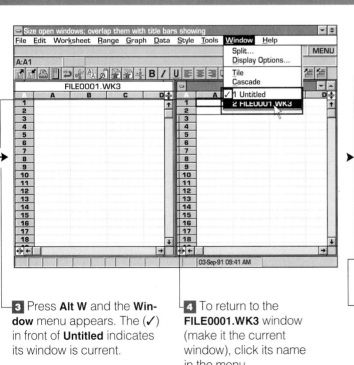

3 Press **Alt W** and the **Window** menu appears. The (✓) in front of **Untitled** indicates its window is current.

4 To return to the **FILE0001.WK3** window (make it the current window), click its name in the menu.

■ The **FILE0001.WK3** window becomes the current window.

Note: Only the current window displays a dark title bar.

HELP

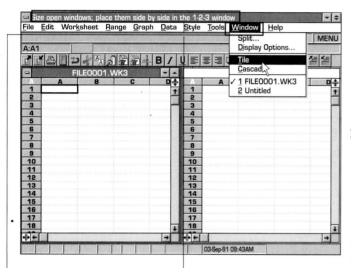

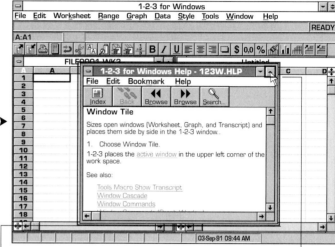

On-line Help provides information on basic skills, commands and procedures.

1 Click a menu title (example: **Window**) to display its commands.

2 Press until the command you want help on is highlighted (example: **Tile**).

■ A brief description of the command appears at the top of the screen.

3 For more information press **F1**.

Note: This procedure can be used for any command listed in the Main menu.

■ The **1-2-3 for Windows Help** window appears.

4 Click the **Maximize** button to enlarge the **1-2-3 for Windows Help** window.

ADDITIONAL NAVIGATION CHOICES

Click this button to view the 1-2-3 for Windows Help Index.

Click this button to move backward through a series of related topics.

Back

Click this button to retrace your path back to the Help Index.

Click this button to move forward through a series of related topics.

Note: When a button dims you have reached the first or last topic in the series.

Click this button to search for information on a specific word or phrase.

USING
THIS GUIDE

START
1 2 3

OPEN A NEW
WORKSHEET FILE

MAXIMIZE
AND RESTORE
A WINDOW

SWITCH
BETWEEN
WINDOWS

HELP

CLOSE
A WINDOW

EXIT
1-2-3

GETTING
STARTED

SMARTICONS

ENTER DATA

SAVE
AND OPEN
WORKSHEETS

MOVE
AND COPY
DATA

ROWS AND
COLUMNS

CHANGE
APPEARANCE
OF DATA

MULTIPLE
WORKSHEET
FILE

CREATE
A GRAPH

PRINT

CREATE A
DATABASE

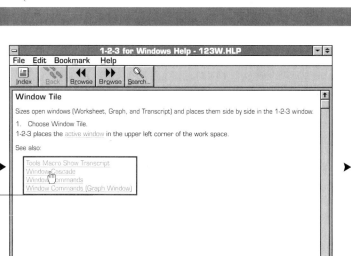

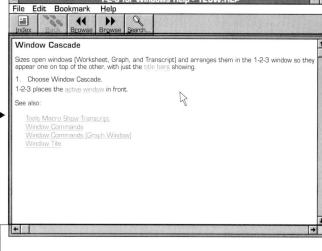

5 Move the mouse ⬉ until it points to a topic (example: **Window Cascade**). The ⬉ turns into a 🖑. Click the left mouse button.

Note: This only applies to dimmed underlined text.

■ A detailed explanation of that topic appears.

6 Point the mouse ⬉ at the next topic of interest and click the left mouse button for more information.

Note: To exit Help, press ***Alt F X****.*

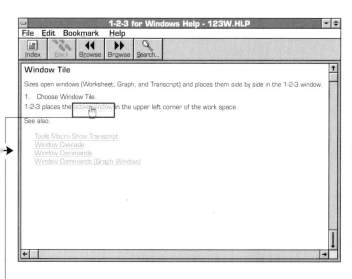

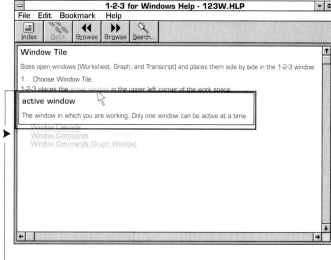

5 Move the mouse ⬉ until it points to a term (example: active window). The ⬉ turns into a 🖑. Click and hold down the left mouse button.

Note: This only applies to dimmed and dotted underlined text.

■ A detailed explanation of that term appears.

Note: To exit Help, press ***Alt F X****.*

CLOSE A WINDOW

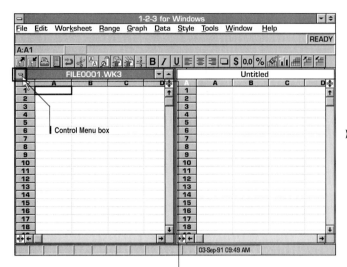

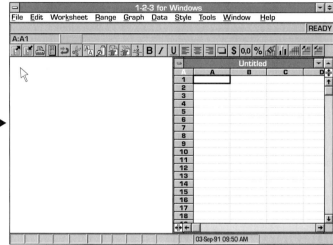

To simplify your workspace, you can close worksheets currently not in use.

1 Move the mouse ⌖ over the **Control Menu box** of **FILE0001.WK3** and click the left button twice in quick succession.

■ The **FILE0001.WK3** window is closed.

USING
THIS GUIDE

START
1-2-3

OPEN A NEW
WORKSHEET FILE

MAXIMIZE
AND RESTORE
A WINDOW

SWITCH
BETWEEN
WINDOWS

HELP

CLOSE
A WINDOW

EXIT
1-2-3

EXIT 1-2-3

GETTING
STARTED

SMARTICONS

ENTER DATA

SAVE
AND OPEN
WORKSHEETS

MOVE
AND COPY
DATA

ROWS AND
COLUMNS

CHANGE
APPEARANCE
OF DATA

MULTIPLE
WORKSHEET
FILE

CREATE
A GRAPH

PRINT

CREATE A
DATABASE

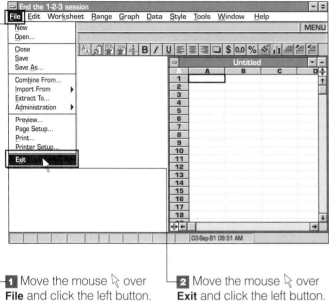

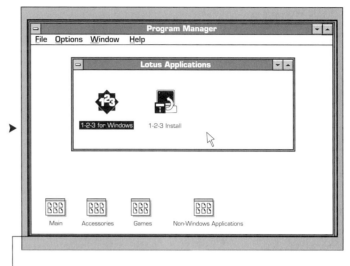

1 Move the mouse ⌷ over **File** and click the left button. The **File** menu appears.

2 Move the mouse ⌷ over **Exit** and click the left button.

Shortcut for Steps 1 and 2

Press **Alt F X**

■ The **Program Manager** window is displayed.

MOUSE VS KEYBOARD

◆ Operations in **1-2-3** are performed using the mouse or keyboard.

◆ For the rest of this guide, we have used either the mouse or the keyboard, depending on which was more efficient for the given operation. In some cases, we have shown both methods.

DESCRIPTIVE SHORTCUTS

For the rest of this guide, the following shortcuts are used:

■ "Move the mouse ⌷ over **xx** and click the left button" becomes

Click xx.

■ "Move the mouse ⌷ over **xx** and click the left button twice in quick succession" becomes

Double click xx.

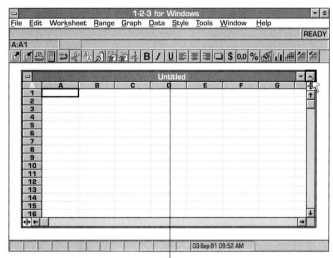

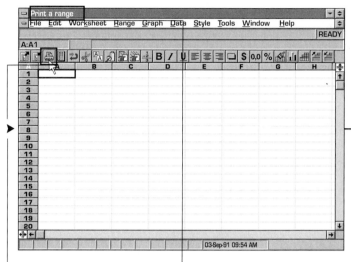

SmartIcons are powerful tools that allow quick and easy access to 1-2-3's most utilized commands.

Note: To start 1-2-3 for Windows, refer to page 4.

1 Move the mouse ▷ over the **Untitled** window's **Maximize** button, and click the left mouse button. This will enlarge your working area.

2 Move the mouse ▷ over any SmartIcon (example: 🖨) and press and hold down the right mouse button.

■ A description of the SmartIcon appears at the top of the screen.

REPOSITION SMARTICONS

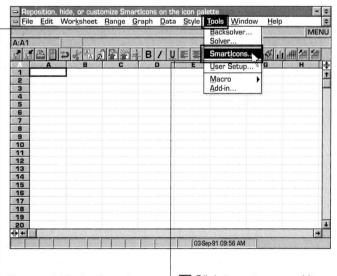

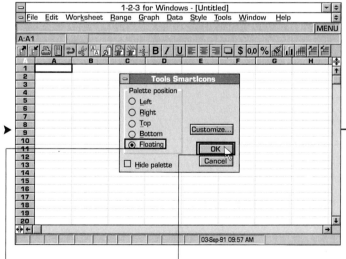

You can hide the SmartIcons or reposition them to the left, right, floating, top or bottom of the screen.

1 Click **Tools** and its menu appears.

2 Click **SmartIcons** and its dialog box appears on the next screen.

Shortcut for Steps 1 and 2

Press **Alt T I**

3 Click the circle beside the desired position of the SmartIcons (○ becomes ◉). For example, select **Floating** so you can manually move and size the SmartIcons.

*Note: To hide the SmartIcons, click the square beside **Hide palette** (☐ becomes ☒).*

4 Click the **OK** button.

GETTING STARTED

SMARTICONS

ENTER DATA

SAVE AND OPEN WORKSHEETS

MOVE AND COPY DATA

ROWS AND COLUMNS

CHANGE APPEARANCE OF DATA

MULTIPLE WORKSHEET FILE

CREATE A GRAPH

PRINT

CREATE A DATABASE

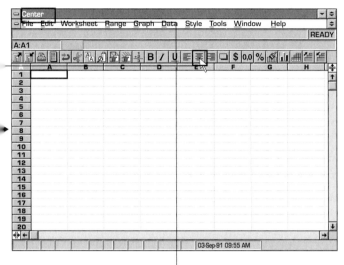

3 Move the mouse ⬚ over another SmartIcon (example: ⬚). Press and hold down the right mouse button.

■ A description of the SmartIcon appears at the top of the screen.

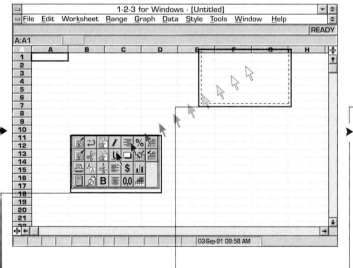

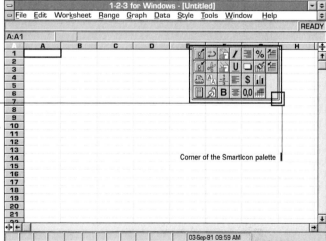

5 To move the SmartIcons to a new location, move the mouse ⬚ over any SmartIcon. Click the left button and hold it down.

6 Still holding down the button, drag the SmartIcons to a new location.

7 Release the button and the SmartIcons are moved.

Note: To resize the SmartIcons, move the mouse ⬚ over any corner of the SmartIcon palette. It turns into ⬚. Click and hold down the button as you drag the edge of the window to the desired size.

ADD A SMARTICON / REMOVE A SMARTICON

ADD A SMARTICON

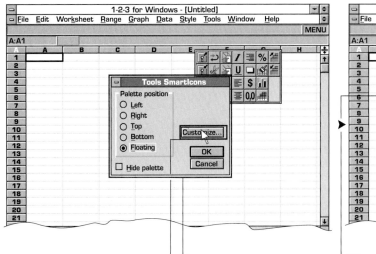

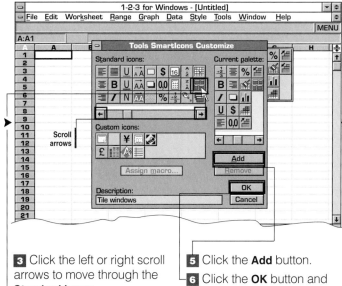

You can customize the SmartIcons to suit your needs.

For example, if you constantly tile windows, add the Tile icon to your screen. Then, tiling can be achieved by one click of the mouse button.

1 Press **Alt T I** (for **T**ools Smart**I**cons) and the **Tools SmartIcons** dialog box appears.

2 Click the **Customize** button and its dialog box appears on the next screen.

3 Click the left or right scroll arrows to move through the **Standard icons**.

4 Click the SmartIcon you want to add to the screen (example: **Tile windows**).

Note: A description of the selected icon appears in the Description box.

5 Click the **Add** button.

6 Click the **OK** button and the **Tools SmartIcons** dialog box appears on the next screen.

REMOVE A SMARTICON

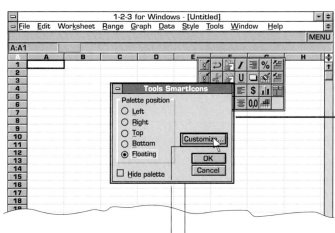

You can easily remove a SmartIcon that you rarely use to help tidy your SmartIcon workspace.

1 Press **Alt T I** and the **Tools SmartIcons** dialog box appears.

2 Click the **Customize** button and its dialog box appears on the next screen.

16 ▶

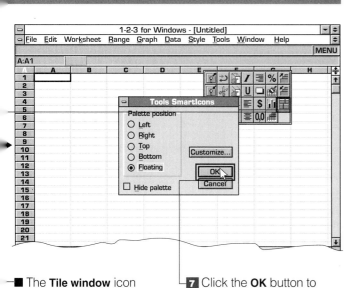

■ The **Tile window** icon appears in the SmartIcon palette.

7 Click the **OK** button to close the **Tools SmartIcons** dialog box.

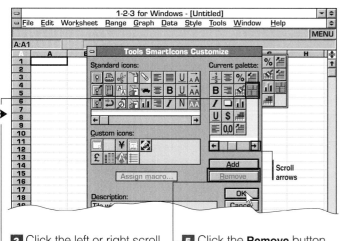

3 Click the left or right scroll arrows to move through the **Current palette** box.

4 Click the SmartIcon you want to delete from your screen (example: **Tile windows**).

5 Click the **Remove** button.

6 Click the **OK** button to close the **Tools SmartIcons Customize** dialog box.

■ The **Tile window** icon is removed from the SmartIcon palette.

7 Click the **OK** button to close the **Tools SmartIcons** dialog box.

*Note: To reposition the SmartIcons to the top of the screen, press **Alt T I** and click the circle beside **Top**. Then press **Enter**.*

GETTING
STARTED

SMARTICONS

ENTER DATA

SAVE
AND OPEN
WORKSHEETS

MOVE
AND COPY
DATA

ROWS AND
COLUMNS

CHANGE
APPEARANCE
OF DATA

MULTIPLE
WORKSHEET
FILE

CREATE
A GRAPH

PRINT

CREATE A
DATABASE

WORKSHEET NAVIGATION

MOVE ONE CELL IN ANY DIRECTION

Press ⬆ to move one cell up.
Press ⬅ to move one cell left.
Press ⬇ to move one cell down.
Press ➡ to move one cell right.

TO MOVE TO THE RIGHT EDGE OF THE WORKSHEET (COLUMN IV)

Press **End** ➡

Note: If data is included in the worksheet, these keys may have to be pressed more than once to get to the desired location.

TO MOVE TO THE BOTTOM EDGE OF THE WORKSHEET (ROW 8192)

Press **End** ⬇

TO MOVE TO THE LOWER RIGHT CORNER OF DATA STORED IN THE WORKSHEET

Press **End Home**

Note: The worksheet must have data in it for this to work.

MOVE TO A1

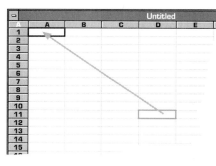

Press **Home** to move to **A1** from anywhere in the worksheet.

MOVE ONE SCREEN UP OR DOWN

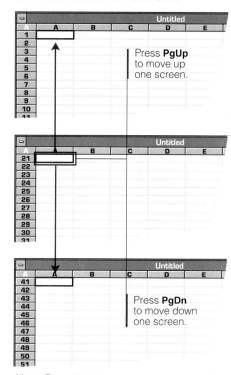

Press **PgUp** to move up one screen.

Press **PgDn** to move down one screen.

Note: Press **Tab** to move one screen to the right. Press **Shift+Tab** to move one screen to the left.

MOVE TO ANY CELL IN THE WORKSHEET

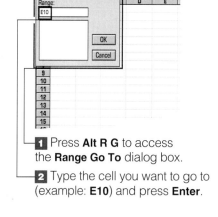

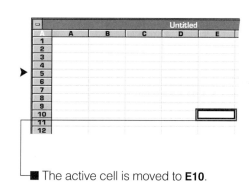

1 Press **Alt R G** to access the **Range Go To** dialog box.

2 Type the cell you want to go to (example: **E10**) and press **Enter**.

■ The active cell is moved to **E10**.

USING THE MOUSE

MOVE TO ANY CELL IN THE WINDOW

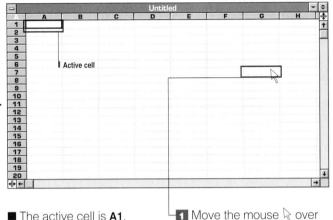

■ The active cell is **A1**.

1 Move the mouse over the cell you want to make active (example: **G7**).

2 Click the left mouse button. The cell **G7** becomes the active cell.

MOVE TO ANY CELL IN THE WORKSHEET *(if the worksheet extends beyond the current window)*

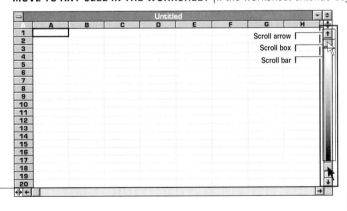

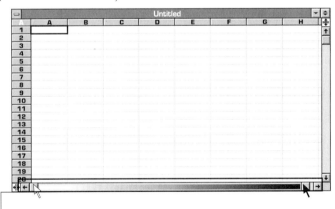

Scroll vertically to the end of the worksheet

1 Move the mouse over the Scroll box. Click the left button and hold it down. Still holding down the button, drag the Scroll box to the end of the Scroll bar. Release the button.

Scroll the screen one line up or down

1 Click the top or bottom scroll arrows.

Scroll horizontally to the end of the worksheet

1 Move the mouse over the Scroll box. Click the left button and hold it down. Still holding down the button, drag the Scroll box to the end of the Scroll bar. Release the button.

Scroll the screen one column right or left

1 Click the left or right scroll arrows.

GETTING STARTED

SMARTICONS

ENTER DATA

SAVE AND OPEN WORKSHEETS

MOVE AND COPY DATA

ROWS AND COLUMNS

CHANGE APPEARANCE OF DATA

MULTIPLE WORKSHEET FILE

CREATE A GRAPH

PRINT

CREATE A DATABASE

RULES
FOR
ENTERING
LABELS

◆ Labels contain text. The text can include letters and/or numbers. The numbers, however, cannot be used in a calculation.

◆ The word LABEL appears in the top right corner of the screen when a label is typed.

◆ The label appears at the left edge of a cell unless otherwise specified by a label prefix.

◆ A label can contain spaces and commas.

◆ A label may not begin with a number or with **+ – $ (# @ ** or **/**, unless preceded by a label prefix.

ENTER LABELS

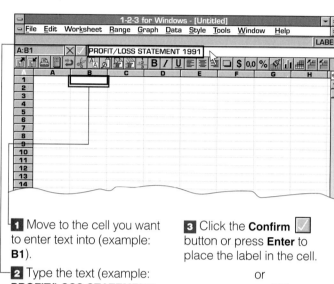

1 Move to the cell you want to enter text into (example: **B1**).

2 Type the text (example: **PROFIT/LOSS STATEMENT 1991**).

1-2-3 knows it is a label because **P**, the first character typed, is a letter.

*Note: If you make a mistake typing, press **Backspace** and retype.*

3 Click the **Confirm** button or press **Enter** to place the label in the cell.

or

Click the **Cancel** button or press **Esc**.

EDIT LABELS AFTER PRESSING ENTER

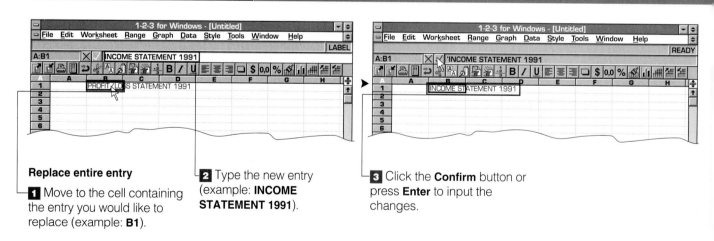

Replace entire entry

1 Move to the cell containing the entry you would like to replace (example: **B1**).

2 Type the new entry (example: **INCOME STATEMENT 1991**).

3 Click the **Confirm** button or press **Enter** to input the changes.

WORKSHEET
NAVIGATION

**ENTER
LABELS**

ENTER NUMBERS
AND FORMULAS

ENTER
FUNCTIONS

SUM USING
THE SMARTICON

GETTING
STARTED

SMARTICONS

ENTER DATA

SAVE
AND OPEN
WORKSHEETS

MOVE
AND COPY
DATA

ROWS AND
COLUMNS

CHANGE
APPEARANCE
OF DATA

MULTIPLE
WORKSHEET
FILE

CREATE
A GRAPH

PRINT

CREATE A
DATABASE

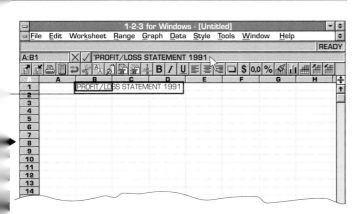

■ The label is entered.

1-2-3 automatically includes the label prefix **'** (apostrophe) when a letter is the first character typed.

*Note: The label prefix **'** is the default setting. It aligns the label to the left edge of the cell.*

Labels that start with numbers

If the first character in a label is a number, type a label prefix before the first character to identify it as a label (example: **'1992 INCOME**).

Label Prefixes

'   Placing **'** before a label aligns it to the left side of the cell.

"   Placing **"** before a label aligns it to the right side of the cell.

^   Placing **^** before a label centers it in the cell.

****   Placing **** before a character (such as a dash) fills the cell with that character.

¦   Placing **¦** before a label in the first cell of a print range tells 1-2-3 not to print that row of data.

Long Labels

◆ If a label is too long to fit into a cell, its text spills over into adjacent cell(s) if they are empty.

◆ If the adjacent cell already contains data, 1-2-3 displays as much of the label as it can. To display the entire label, the column must be widened. (Refer to page 44.)

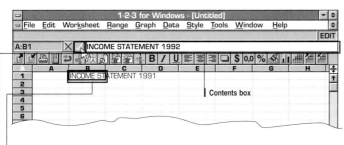

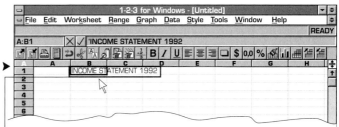

Edit minor changes to entry using the mouse

1 Move to the cell with the incorrect entry (example: **B1**).

2 In the **Contents** box, drag the mouse (it changes from ▷ to ⌶) over the character(s) to be replaced (example: **199⬛**). Type the correction (example: **2**).

3 Click the **Confirm** button to enter the changes.

Note: To use the keyboard

*1. Move to the cell containing the incorrect entry and press **F2** (the Edit key).*

*2. Move the cursor to the point of change and press **Backspace** to delete unwanted characters. Type the correction.*

*3. Press **Enter** to input the changes.*

■ The change is displayed.

Edit key descriptions when in Contents box

Home	-	Move to the beginning of the data.
End	-	Move to the end of the data.
⬅ or ➡	-	Move one character in the direction of the arrow.
Backspace	-	Deletes the character to the left of the cursor.

ENTER NUMBERS AND FORMULAS

ORDER OF PRECEDENCE

◆ Mathematical operators are included in formulas:

+	Add	–	Subtract
*	Multiply	/	Divide

◆ 1-2-3 performs operations in formulas based on the order of precedence.

Operation	Order of Precedence
Multiplication Division	1 1 } Done in order of appearance
Addition Subtraction	2 2 } Done in order of appearance
Example:	15–3*4 is executed as follows: –3*4+15=3
Example:	18/2*3 is executed as follows: 18/2*3=27
Example:	1+2+3*4 is executed as follows: 3*4+1+2=15

Overriding the order of precedence

To override the order of precedence, parenthesis can be used:

Examples:

Formula	Execution
E5–E7*E9 (E5–E7)*E9	15–3*4=3 (15–3)*4=48
+G5/H2*H7 G5/(H2*H7)	18/2*3=27 18/(2*3)=3
J5+J6+J7+J9 (J5+J6+J7)*J9	1+2+3*4=15 (1+2+3)*4=24

WORKSHEET
NAVIGATION

ENTER
LABELS

**ENTER NUMBERS
AND FORMULAS**

ENTER
FUNCTIONS

SUM USING
THE SMARTICON

GETTING
STARTED

SMARTICONS

ENTER DATA

SAVE
AND OPEN
WORKSHEETS

MOVE
AND COPY
DATA

ROWS AND
COLUMNS

CHANGE
APPEARANCE
OF DATA

MULTIPLE
WORKSHEET
FILE

CREATE
A GRAPH

PRINT

CREATE A
DATABASE

◆ A formula performs calculations and contains mathematical operators, numbers and cell addresses.

◆ A formula begins with a number (0 through 9) or symbol + – (@ .

◆ The formula appears at the top of the screen when the cell pointer is at the cell containing the formula (example: B11).

◆ Cell addresses are used so that if the data in a cell changes, a formula somewhere else in the worksheet will not have to be altered.

◆ The result of the calculation appears at the cell containing the formula (example: B11).

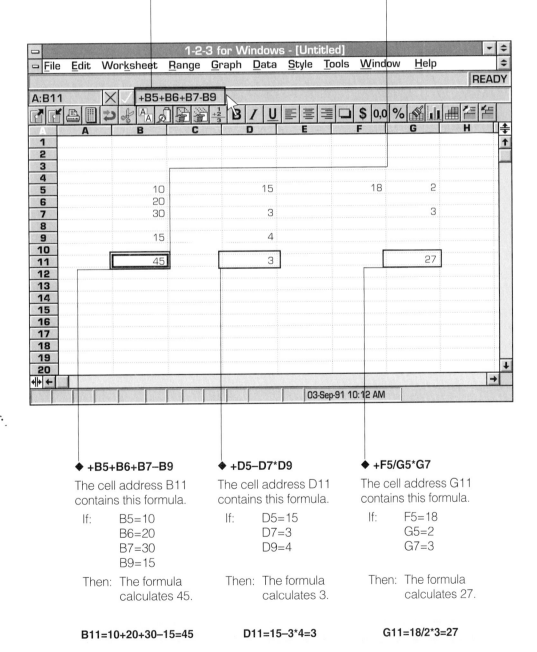

◆ **+B5+B6+B7–B9**

The cell address B11 contains this formula.

If: B5=10
     B6=20
     B7=30
     B9=15

Then: The formula
      calculates 45.

B11=10+20+30–15=45

◆ **+D5–D7*D9**

The cell address D11 contains this formula.

If: D5=15
     D7=3
     D9=4

Then: The formula
      calculates 3.

D11=15–3*4=3

◆ **+F5/G5*G7**

The cell address G11 contains this formula.

If: F5=18
     G5=2
     G7=3

Then: The formula
      calculates 27.

G11=18/2*3=27

ENTER NUMBERS
AND FORMULAS

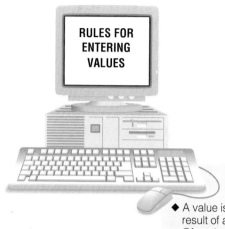

RULES FOR
ENTERING
VALUES

ENTER NUMBERS

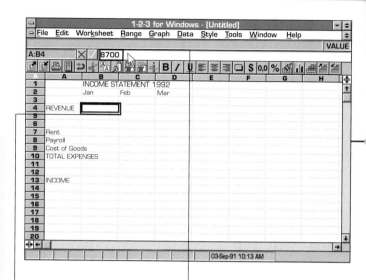

◆ A value is a number or the result of a formula or @function.

◆ The word VALUE appears in the top right corner of the screen when a value is typed.

◆ A value appears at the right edge of a cell. Its position cannot be changed.

◆ A value begins with a number (0 through 9) or an operator + – (@ . $.

◆ A value can only contain one decimal point.

1 Select the cell you want to enter a number into (example: **B4**).

Note: Row and column headings have been added to the worksheet.

2 Type the number (example: **8700**).

ENTER FORMULAS

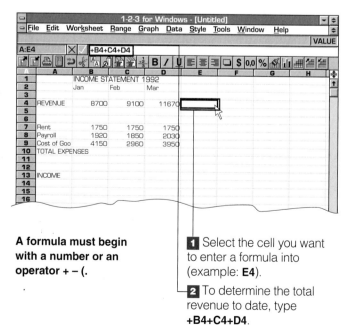

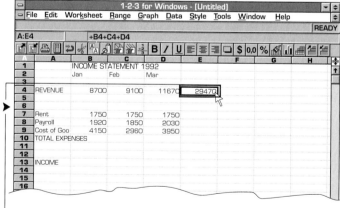

A formula must begin with a number or an operator + – (.

1 Select the cell you want to enter a formula into (example: **E4**).

2 To determine the total revenue to date, type **+B4+C4+D4**.

3 Press **Enter** and the calculation is displayed.

24 ▶

WORKSHEET
NAVIGATION

ENTER
LABELS

**ENTER NUMBERS
AND FORMULAS**

ENTER
FUNCTIONS

SUM USING
THE SMARTICON

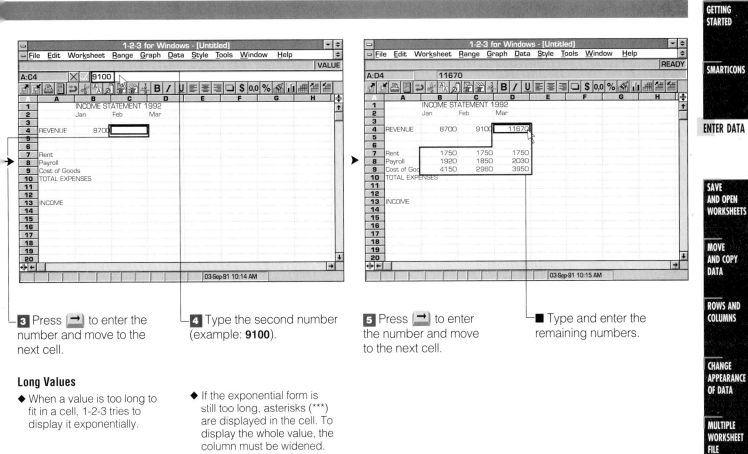

3 Press → to enter the number and move to the next cell.

4 Type the second number (example: **9100**).

5 Press → to enter the number and move to the next cell.

■ Type and enter the remaining numbers.

Long Values

◆ When a value is too long to fit in a cell, 1-2-3 tries to display it exponentially.

◆ If the exponential form is still too long, asterisks (***) are displayed in the cell. To display the whole value, the column must be widened.

AUTOMATIC RECALCULATION

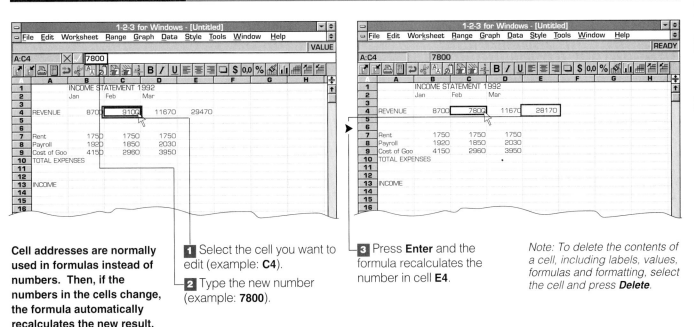

Cell addresses are normally used in formulas instead of numbers. Then, if the numbers in the cells change, the formula automatically recalculates the new result.

1 Select the cell you want to edit (example: **C4**).

2 Type the new number (example: **7800**).

3 Press **Enter** and the formula recalculates the number in cell **E4**.

*Note: To delete the contents of a cell, including labels, values, formulas and formatting, select the cell and press **Delete**.*

GETTING STARTED

SMARTICONS

ENTER DATA

SAVE AND OPEN WORKSHEETS

MOVE AND COPY DATA

ROWS AND COLUMNS

CHANGE APPEARANCE OF DATA

MULTIPLE WORKSHEET FILE

CREATE A GRAPH

PRINT

CREATE A DATABASE

ENTER FUNCTIONS

@Functions are formulas built into 1-2-3 to perform time-saving set-up procedures.

Although there are many kinds of @Functions, they all follow the same basic rules.

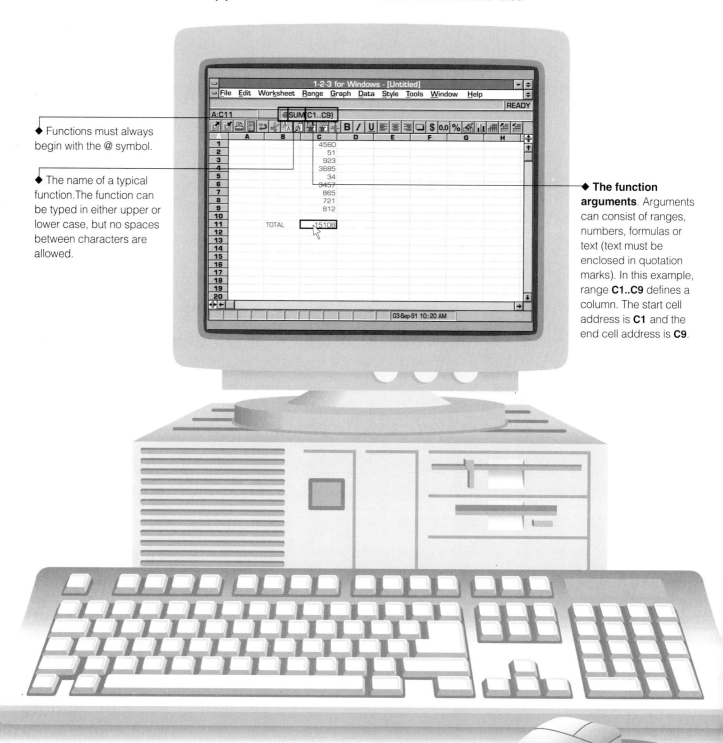

◆ Functions must always begin with the @ symbol.

◆ The name of a typical function. The function can be typed in either upper or lower case, but no spaces between characters are allowed.

◆ **The function arguments.** Arguments can consist of ranges, numbers, formulas or text (text must be enclosed in quotation marks). In this example, range **C1..C9** defines a column. The start cell address is **C1** and the end cell address is **C9**.

WORKSHEET
NAVIGATION

ENTER
LABELS

ENTER NUMBERS
AND FORMULAS

**ENTER
FUNCTIONS**

SUM USING
THE SMARTICON

GETTING
STARTED

SMARTICONS

ENTER DATA

SAVE
AND OPEN
WORKSHEETS

MOVE
AND COPY
DATA

ROWS AND
COLUMNS

CHANGE
APPEARANCE
OF DATA

MULTIPLE
WORKSHEET
FILE

CREATE
A GRAPH

PRINT

CREATE A
DATABASE

TYPICAL @FUNCTIONS

@SUM - Adds together the data in a range of cells.
Example: @SUM(C1..C9)

@ROUND - Rounds any value up to 15 decimal places.
Example: @ROUND(C2,1) where "1" is the number of decimal places

@DATE - Calculates the serial date number for any date after Dec 31,1899.
Example: @DATE(92,03,01) for March 1, 1992 = 33664

@MAX - Finds the largest value in a list of numbers.
Example: @MAX(B2..B70)

@AVG - Averages the values of numbers or ranges.
Example: @AVG(B1..B6)

@MIN - Finds the minimum value in a list of numbers.
Example: @MIN(B2..B70)

Note: For a complete list of @Functions, refer to the Lotus User's Guide.

SELECT A RANGE

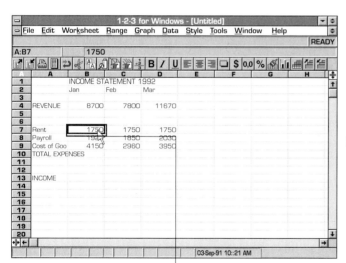

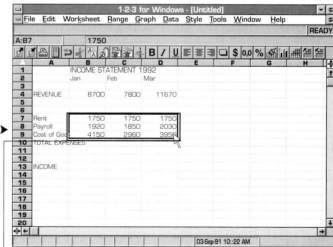

To perform a function a range must be specified. A range is a rectangular block of cells that 1-2-3 treats as a unit. Ranges allow 1-2-3 to copy, move, sort, print and delete information efficiently.

1 Move to the first cell that you want to select (example: **B7**).

2 Click the left button and hold it down.

3 Still holding down the button, drag the mouse to the diagonally opposite corner of the range you want to select (example: **D9**). Then release the button.

Note: A range can only be square or rectangular in shape.

To Cancel a Range Selection

Click anywhere on the worksheet.

ENTER FUNCTIONS

@SUM FUNCTION

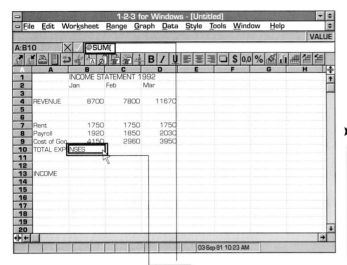
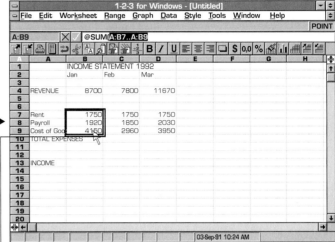

Add the range of cells B7 to B9 and place the sum in cell B10.

1 Select the cell you want to enter the SUM function into (example: **B10**).

2 Type the function and an open parenthesis. For example: **@SUM(**

3 Use the mouse to select the range of cells you want to sum (example: **B7** to **B9**).

To Cancel a Function

Press **Esc**.

*Note: To specify a range using the keyboard, type the top left cell address followed by a • (period) and then the bottom right cell address (example: **B7.B9**).*

When you type a range, only one • (period) is required. When 1-2-3 identifies a range, it uses two periods (..).

@DATE FUNCTION

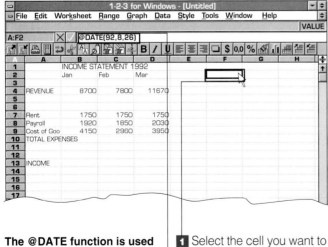
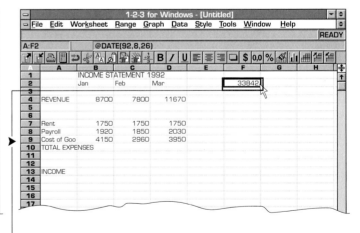

The @DATE function is used to key dates into a worksheet that will later be used for sorting, or calculating elapsed time.

The keying sequence is @DATE(YY,MM,DD).

1 Select the cell you want to enter the DATE function into (example: **F2**).

2 To key in August 26, 1992 type **@DATE(92,8,26)**.

3 Press **Enter** and a serial date number of **33842** (the number of days since January 1, 1900) is placed in cell **F2**.

Note: Elapsed time can be calculated by subtracting two DATE functions.

*Note: If **ERR** (error) appears in the cell, check the entry for typing errors.*

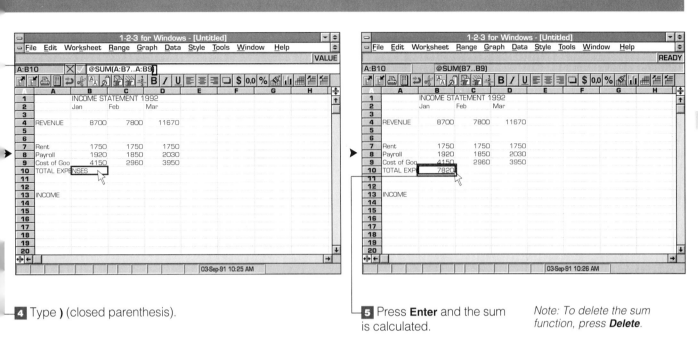

4 Type **)** (closed parenthesis).

5 Press **Enter** and the sum is calculated.

*Note: To delete the sum function, press **Delete**.*

DELETE A FUNCTION

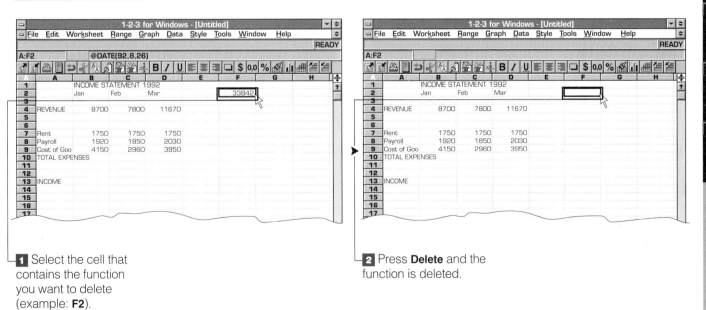

1 Select the cell that contains the function you want to delete (example: **F2**).

2 Press **Delete** and the function is deleted.

GETTING STARTED

SMARTICONS

ENTER DATA

SAVE AND OPEN WORKSHEETS

MOVE AND COPY DATA

ROWS AND COLUMNS

CHANGE APPEARANCE OF DATA

MULTIPLE WORKSHEET FILE

CREATE A GRAPH

PRINT

CREATE A DATABASE

SUM USING
THE SMARTICON

SUM A SINGLE COLUMN (or row)

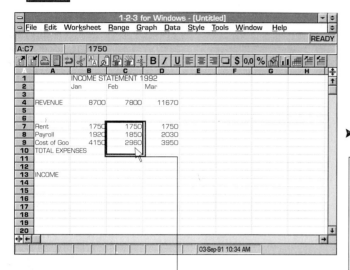 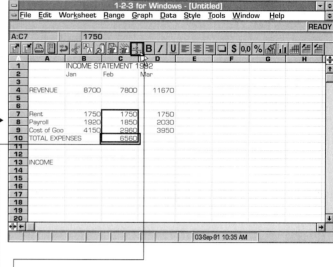

The Sum SmartIcon can add a single column or row.

1 Select the column you want to sum, and the adjacent cell which will display the sum.

2 Click the **Sum** SmartIcon.

■ The sum of the column is displayed.

Note: The same method can be used to sum a single row.

SUM MULTIPLE ROWS AND COLUMNS

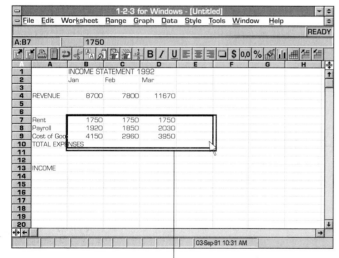 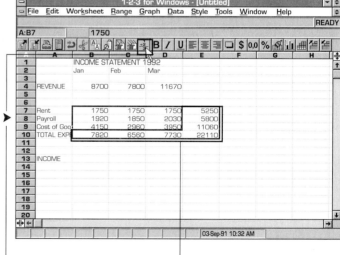

The Sum SmartIcon can add multiple rows and columns and place the results in adjacent cells.

1 Select the rows and columns you want to sum, and the adjacent cells which will display the sum.

Note: To select a range, refer to page 27.

2 Click the **Sum** SmartIcon.

■ The row and column sums are displayed.

*Note: To undo the summation, click the **Undo** SmartIcon.*

GETTING STARTED

SMARTICONS

ENTER DATA

SAVE AND OPEN WORKSHEETS

MOVE AND COPY DATA

ROWS AND COLUMNS

CHANGE APPEARANCE OF DATA

MULTIPLE WORKSHEET FILE

CREATE A GRAPH

PRINT

CREATE A DATABASE

UNDO

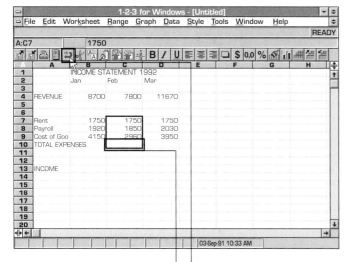

IMPORTANT

The Undo command is off when you first install 1-2-3. To turn it on press Alt T U and click the square beside Enable Edit Undo (☐ becomes ☒). Then press Enter.

The Undo SmartIcon cancels your last command. This only works immediately after a command is used.

1 Click the **Undo** SmartIcon.

■ The summation is removed from the column.

1+2/3 SUM MULTIPLE COLUMNS (or rows)

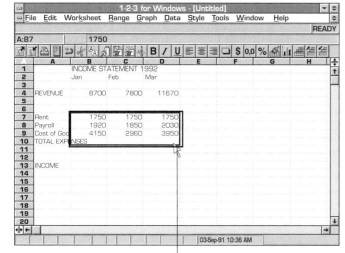

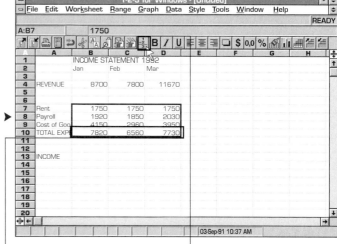

The Sum SmartIcon can add multiple columns or rows.

1 Select the multiple columns you want to sum, and the adjacent cells which will display their sums.

2 Click the **Sum** SmartIcon.

■ The sum of each column is displayed.

Note: The same method can be used to sum multiple rows.

FILES AND DIRECTORIES

HOW FILES ARE SPECIFIED

In an efficient and productive office environment, people create, edit, review and organize paper documents (example: letters, worksheets, reports, etc.). These documents are stored in folders, which in turn are placed in cabinets. To retrieve a specific document, you must identify it by location (cabinet and folder) and then by name.

Computers work the same way. After creating a document in 1-2-3, it must be named and saved. During the save process, you must tell 1-2-3 the directory (folder) and drive (cabinet) the file is to reside in.

In 1-2-3 there is a multilevel directory filing system to store and retrieve your programs. The first level of this directory structure is called the root directory. From this directory other subdirectories can be created. A typical multilevel filing system is illustrated on the next page.

To create or delete sub-directories refer to your Windows User Guide.

Note: The terms "directory" and "subdirectory" are used interchangeably. The "root directory" is the only "directory" that cannot be called a "subdirectory".

FILE SPECIFICATION

A file is specified by describing its drive, path and name (filename and extension).

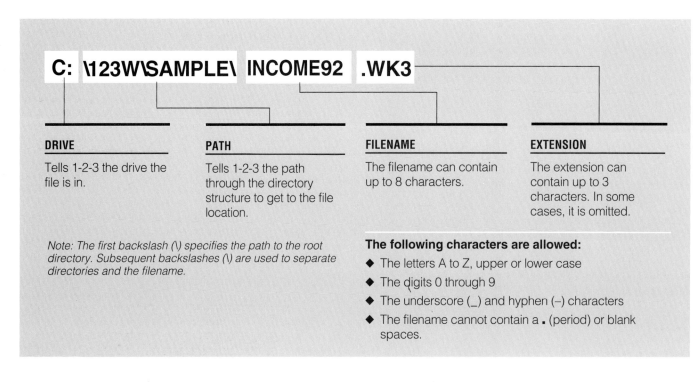

C: \123W\SAMPLE\ INCOME92 .WK3

DRIVE

Tells 1-2-3 the drive the file is in.

PATH

Tells 1-2-3 the path through the directory structure to get to the file location.

FILENAME

The filename can contain up to 8 characters.

EXTENSION

The extension can contain up to 3 characters. In some cases, it is omitted.

Note: The first backslash (\) specifies the path to the root directory. Subsequent backslashes (\) are used to separate directories and the filename.

The following characters are allowed:

◆ The letters A to Z, upper or lower case

◆ The digits 0 through 9

◆ The underscore (_) and hyphen (–) characters

◆ The filename cannot contain a **.** (period) or blank spaces.

USING DIRECTORIES TO ORGANIZE YOUR FILES

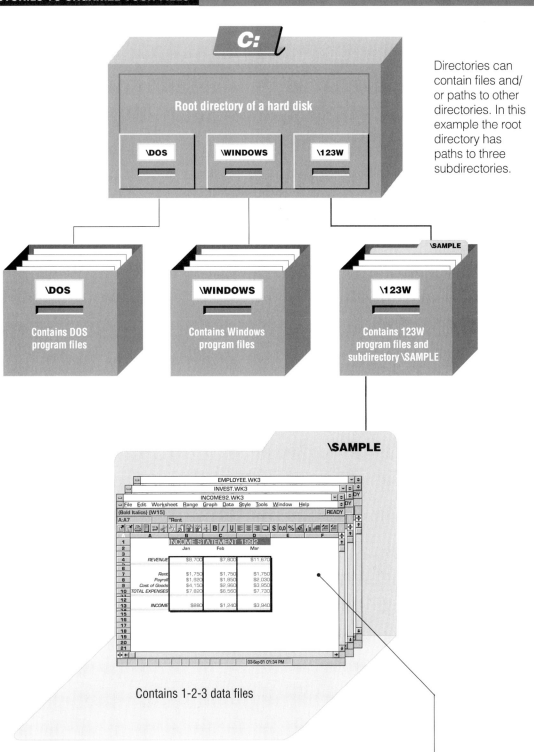

Directories can contain files and/or paths to other directories. In this example the root directory has paths to three subdirectories.

Root directory of a hard disk

\DOS | \WINDOWS | \123W

\SAMPLE

\DOS
Contains DOS program files

\WINDOWS
Contains Windows program files

\123W
Contains 123W program files and subdirectory \SAMPLE

\SAMPLE

Contains 1-2-3 data files

The file specification for this data file is:

C:\123W\SAMPLE\INCOME92.WK3

GETTING STARTED

SMARTICONS

ENTER DATA

SAVE AND OPEN WORKSHEETS

MOVE AND COPY DATA

ROWS AND COLUMNS

CHANGE APPEARANCE OF DATA

MULTIPLE WORKSHEET FILE

CREATE A GRAPH

PRINT

CREATE A DATABASE

SAVE
A WORKSHEET
FILE

All examples in this guide are based on the directory structure illustrated below:

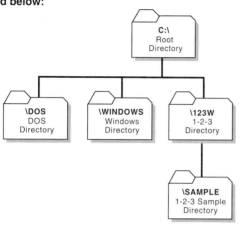

SAVE A NEW WORKSHEET FILE

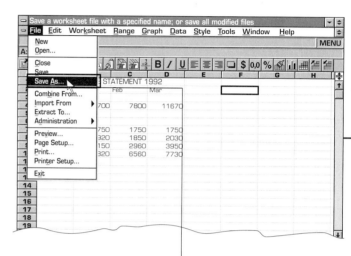

The worksheet must be saved before leaving 1-2-3 if it is required for future use.

Save worksheet to SAMPLE directory and give it a name.

1 Click **File** to open its menu.

2 Click **Save As** and the **File Save As** dialog box appears on the next screen.

Shortcut for Steps 1 and 2

Press **Alt F A**

SAVE A WORKSHEET FILE USING A DIFFERENT NAME

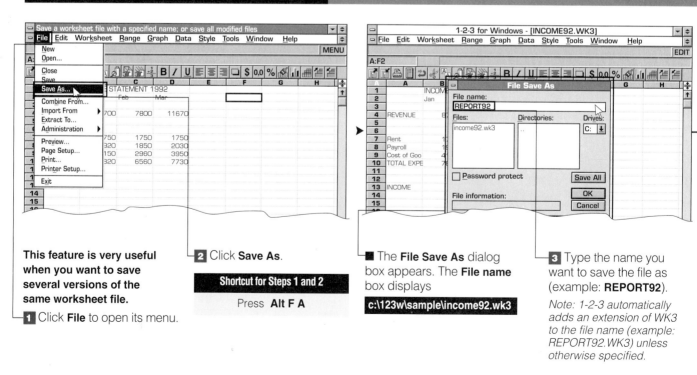

This feature is very useful when you want to save several versions of the same worksheet file.

1 Click **File** to open its menu.

2 Click **Save As**.

Shortcut for Steps 1 and 2

Press **Alt F A**

■ The **File Save As** dialog box appears. The **File name** box displays

c:\123w\sample\income92.wk3

3 Type the name you want to save the file as (example: **REPORT92**).

Note: 1-2-3 automatically adds an extension of WK3 to the file name (example: REPORT92.WK3) unless otherwise specified.

FILES AND
DIRECTORIES

**SAVE
A WORKSHEET
FILE**

OPEN
A WORKSHEET
FILE

GETTING
STARTED

SMARTICONS

ENTER DATA

**SAVE
AND OPEN
WORKSHEETS**

MOVE
AND COPY
DATA

ROWS AND
COLUMNS

CHANGE
APPEARANCE
OF DATA

MULTIPLE
WORKSHEET
FILE

CREATE
A GRAPH

PRINT

CREATE A
DATABASE

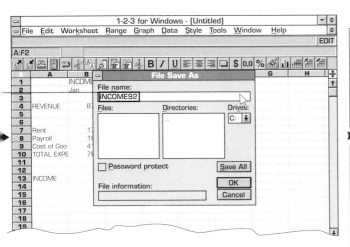

■ The File name box displays

`c:\123w\sample\file0001.wk3`

3 Type the name that you
want to save the file as
(example: **INCOME92**). It
replaces the original file name
c:\123w\sample\file0001.wk3.

*Note: 1-2-3 automatically
adds an extension of WK3 to
the file name (example:
INCOME92.WK3) unless
otherwise specified.*

4 Press **Enter** and the
worksheet **INCOME92.WK3** is
saved to the **SAMPLE**
directory.

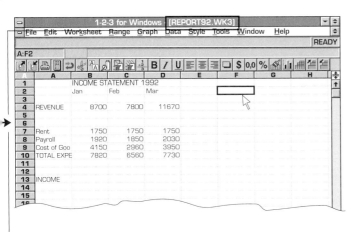

4 Press **Enter** and the
worksheet **REPORT92.WK3**
is saved.

*Note: The worksheet
INCOME92.WK3 is still on the
hard drive.*

**SAVE A WORKSHEET
USING THIS SMARTICON**

Click the **Save** SmartIcon to
quickly save your worksheet
to the current directory,
using the same name.

CAUTION

The worksheet will
replace the previously
saved worksheet.

*Note: You should save
regularly to prevent losing
work due to power failure or
hardware malfunctions.*

SAVE A WORKSHEET FILE

OPEN A WORKSHEET FILE

SAVE A WORKSHEET FILE TO A FLOPPY DRIVE USING THE SAME NAME

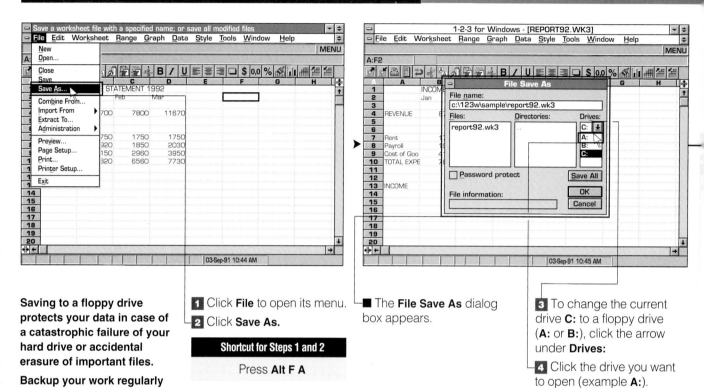

Saving to a floppy drive protects your data in case of a catastrophic failure of your hard drive or accidental erasure of important files.

Backup your work regularly (daily or weekly).

1 Click **File** to open its menu.

2 Click **Save As**.

Shortcut for Steps 1 and 2

Press **Alt F A**

■ The **File Save As** dialog box appears.

3 To change the current drive **C:** to a floppy drive (**A:** or **B:**), click the arrow under **Drives:**

4 Click the drive you want to open (example **A:**).

OPEN A WORKSHEET FILE FROM THE SAMPLE DIRECTORY

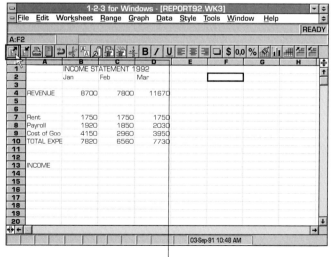

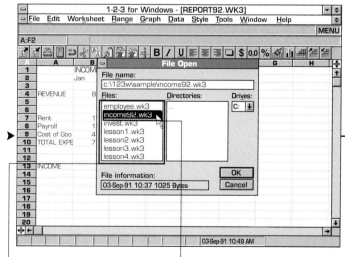

Let us assume you created a document in 1-2-3, named it INCOME92 and saved it to the SAMPLE directory.

1 Click the **Open File** SmartIcon.

■ The **SAMPLE** directory files are displayed in the **Files** box.

*Note: The **File Information** box displays the date the file was last modified and its size.*

2 Click the name of the file you want to open (example: **INCOME92.WK3**).

FILES AND
DIRECTORIES

SAVE
A WORKSHEET
FILE

OPEN
A WORKSHEET
FILE

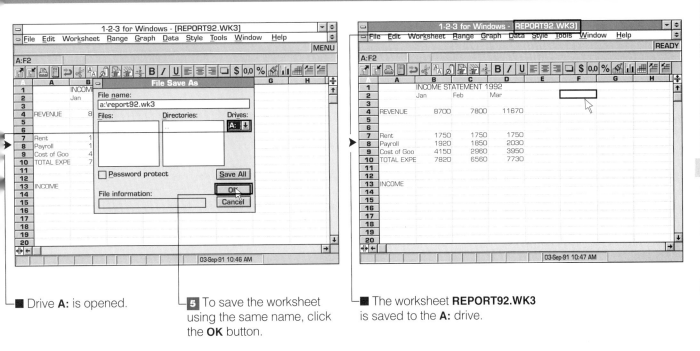

■ Drive **A:** is opened.

5 To save the worksheet using the same name, click the **OK** button.

■ The worksheet **REPORT92.WK3** is saved to the **A:** drive.

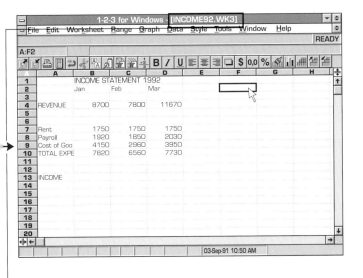

3 Press **Enter** to open the **INCOME92.WK3** worksheet.

GETTING
STARTED

SMARTICONS

ENTER DATA

SAVE
AND OPEN
WORKSHEETS

MOVE
AND COPY
DATA

ROWS AND
COLUMNS

CHANGE
APPEARANCE
OF DATA

MULTIPLE
WORKSHEET
FILE

CREATE
A GRAPH

PRINT

CREATE A
DATABASE

MOVE DATA

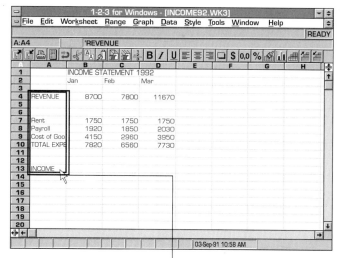

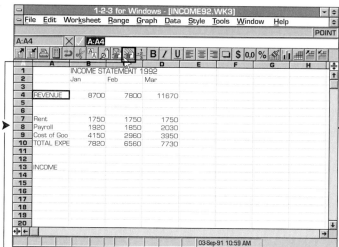

You can move data from a cell range to a new location using the Move SmartIcon.

1 Select the range of cells (example: **A4.A13**) you want to move to a new location.

2 Click the **Move** SmartIcon and the mouse turns into .

MOVE DATA USING THE CLIPBOARD

The clipboard is a temporary storage area which retains the data to be moved. The data remains on the clipboard until you cut or copy the next cell range.

The clipboard is useful when moving data in a multiple worksheet file or to another windows application.

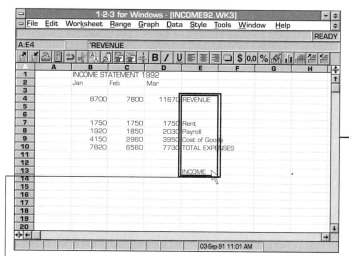

1 Select the range of cells (example: **E4.E13**) you want to move to a new location.

GETTING STARTED

SMARTICONS

ENTER DATA

SAVE AND OPEN WORKSHEETS

MOVE AND COPY DATA

ROWS AND COLUMNS

CHANGE APPEARANCE OF DATA

MULTIPLE WORKSHEET FILE

CREATE A GRAPH

PRINT

CREATE A DATABASE

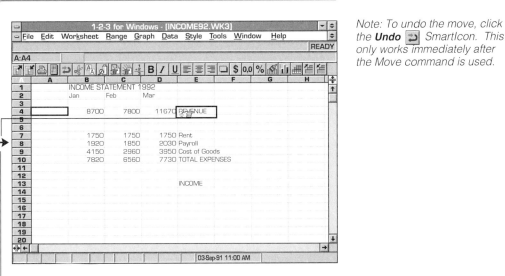

*Note: To undo the move, click the **Undo** ⟳ SmartIcon. This only works immediately after the Move command is used.*

3 Click the cell (example: **E4**) you want to move the data to.

Note: The selected cell is used as the top left corner cell of the new location.

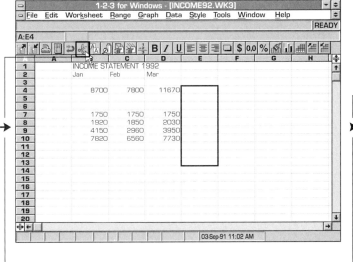

2 Click the **Cut** SmartIcon and the data is removed and copied to the clipboard.

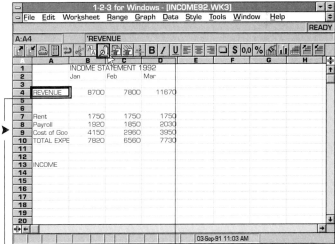

3 Click the cell (example: **A4**) you want 1-2-3 to move the data to.

Note: The selected cell is used as the top left corner cell of the new location.

4 Click the **Paste** SmartIcon and the data is moved to the new location.

*Note: To undo the move, click the **Undo** ⟳ SmartIcon. This only works immediately after the Move command is used.*

COPY DATA

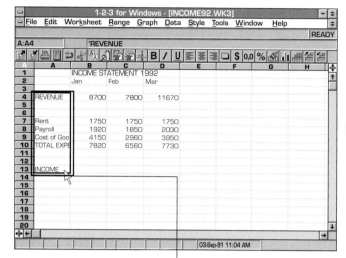

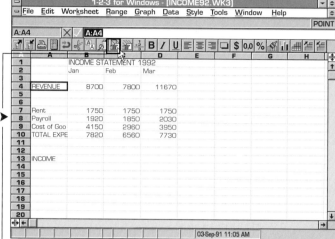

You can copy data from a cell range to a new location using the Copy SmartIcon.

1 Select the range of cells (example: **A4.A13**) you want to copy to a new location.

2 Click the **Copy** SmartIcon and the mouse turns into a pointer.

COPY DATA USING THE CLIPBOARD

The clipboard is a temporary storage area which retains the data to be copied. The data remains on the clipboard until you cut or copy the next cell range.

The clipboard is useful when copying data in a multiple worksheet file or to another windows application.

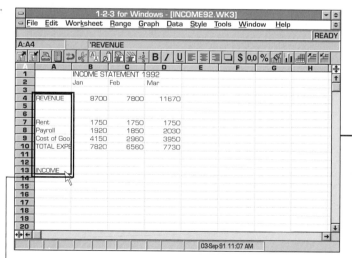

1 Select the range of cells (example: **A4.A13**) you want to copy to a new location.

GETTING
STARTED

SMARTICONS

ENTER DATA

SAVE
AND OPEN
WORKSHEETS

MOVE
AND COPY
DATA

ROWS AND
COLUMNS

CHANGE
APPEARANCE
OF DATA

MULTIPLE
WORKSHEET
FILE

CREATE
A GRAPH

PRINT

CREATE A
DATABASE

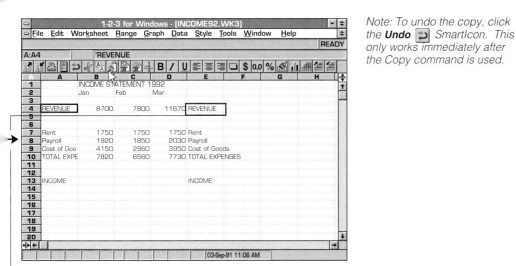

*Note: To undo the copy, click
the* **Undo** *SmartIcon. This
only works immediately after
the Copy command is used.*

3 Click the cell you want
to copy the data to
(example: **E4**).

*Note: The selected cell is used
as the top left corner cell of the
new location.*

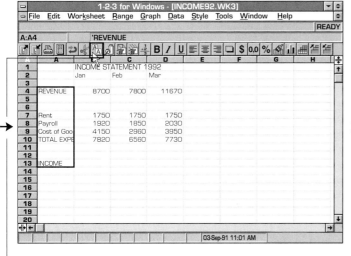

2 Click the **Copy to the
Clipboard** SmartIcon and
the data is copied to the
clipboard.

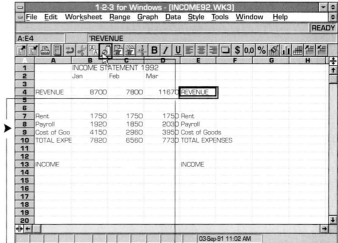

3 Click the cell
(example: **E4**) you want
1-2-3 to copy the data to.

*Note: The selected cell is used
as the top left corner cell of the
new location.*

4 Click the **Paste** SmartIcon
and the data is copied to the
new location.

*Note: To undo the copy, click
the* **Undo** *SmartIcon. This
only works immediately after
the Copy command is used.*

COPY DATA USING RELATIVE REFERENCES

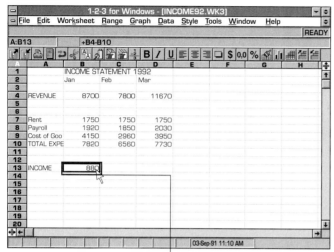

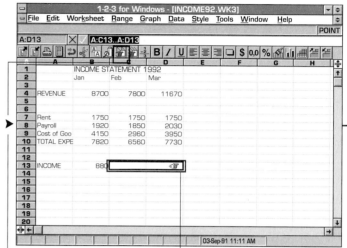

1-2-3 remembers cell addresses in a relative way. If a formula is copied to a range of cells, the cell references adjust automatically.

1 Select the cell (example: **B13**) that contains the formula you want to copy to other cells.

Note: The formula +B4-B10 was entered into cell B13 to determine Income.

2 Click the **Copy** SmartIcon and the mouse ☝ turns into ☞ .

3 Select the cells (example: **C13.D13**) you want to copy the formula to.

COPY DATA USING ABSOLUTE REFERENCES

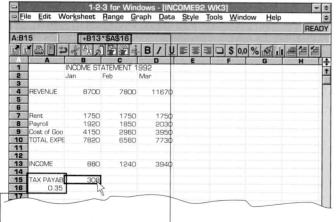

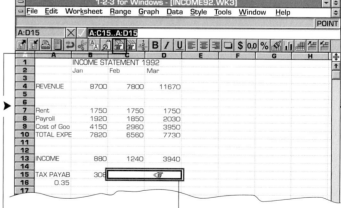

If a formula contains an absolute reference, 1-2-3 will not change the cell or range address when you copy the formula.

1 Enter data to be used as an absolute cell reference (example: **0.35** in cell **A16**).

2 Enter the formula containing the absolute reference (example: **+B13*A16**).

Note: The $ signs tell 1-2-3 that cell A16 is an absolute cell reference. This means the value of cell A16(0.35) is fixed during the copying process.

3 Click the **Copy** SmartIcon and the mouse ☝ turns into ☞ .

4 Select the cells (example: **C15.D15**) you want to copy the formula to.

GETTING STARTED

SMARTICONS

ENTER DATA

SAVE AND OPEN WORKSHEETS

MOVE AND COPY DATA

ROWS AND COLUMNS

CHANGE APPEARANCE OF DATA

MULTIPLE WORKSHEET FILE

CREATE A GRAPH

PRINT

CREATE A DATABASE

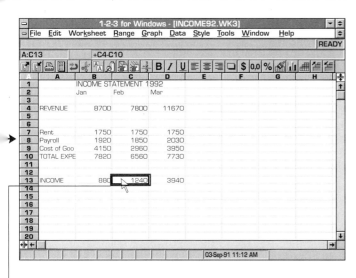

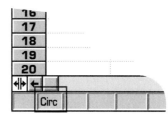

If **Circ** appears, the formula you just entered is included within its own range.

Always remove the Circular Reference before continuing.

To locate the cell containing the Circular Reference press **Alt H A**.

■ Press [→] to move one cell to the right.

Note: The formulas are adjusted and recalculated for the months of February and March.

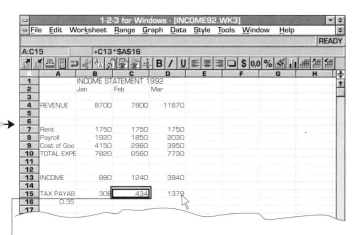

■ Press [→] to move one cell to the right.

Note: The formulas are adjusted and recalculated for the months of February and March.

Copying Cells With Absolute Cell References

Example: +B13*A16

The first $ sign tells 1-2-3 that the column in the cell reference address is fixed. The second $ sign tells 1-2-3 that the row in the cell reference address is also fixed during the copy process.

CHANGE COLUMN WIDTH

USING THE MOUSE TO CHANGE COLUMN WIDTH

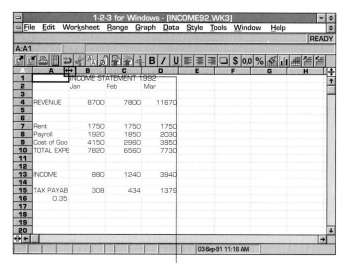

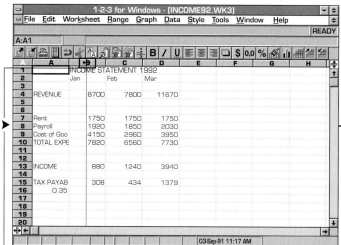

You may want to change the column width to enhance your worksheet or display hidden data.

When a value is too long to fit in a cell, 1-2-3 displays *** (asterisks) across the cell. When a label is too long to fit in a cell, 1-2-3 displays as much of the label as it can if the adjacent cell already contains data.

In this example, we will change the width of column A.

1 Move the mouse ▷ to the right edge of the column heading and it changes to ↔.

2 Hold down the left button and drag the border to the desired width.

Note: Increasing or decreasing the column width changes the number of columns visible.

CHANGE COLUMN WIDTH ACROSS ENTIRE WORKSHEET

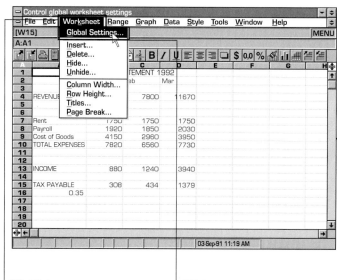

1 Click **Worksheet** and its menu appears.

2 Click **Global Settings**.

Shortcut for Steps 1 and 2

Press **Alt K G**

CHANGE
COLUMN WIDTH   CHANGE
ROW HEIGHT   INSERT A ROW
OR COLUMN   DELETE A ROW
OR COLUMN

GETTING
STARTED

SMARTICONS

ENTER DATA

SAVE
AND OPEN
WORKSHEETS

MOVE
AND COPY
DATA

ROWS AND
COLUMNS

CHANGE
APPEARANCE
OF DATA

MULTIPLE
WORKSHEET
FILE

CREATE
A GRAPH

PRINT

CREATE A
DATABASE

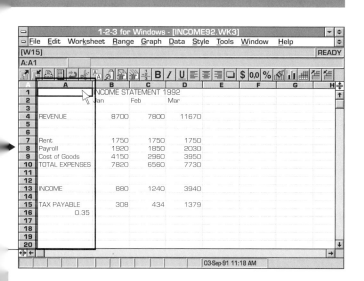

3 Release the button and the width of column **A** is changed.

*Note: To reset the column width to its original setting, press **Alt K C**. The **Worksheet Column Width** dialog box appears. Click the circle next to **Reset to global** (○ becomes ◉). Then press **Enter**.*

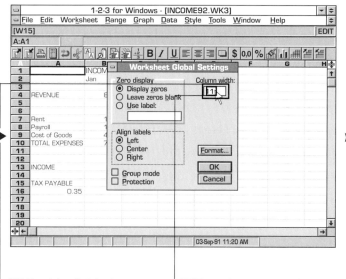

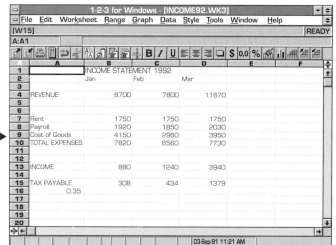

3 Double click in the **Column width** box.

4 Type the number of characters you want to fit into each column (example: **11**).

5 Press **Enter** and the column width across the entire worksheet is changed to accommodate 11 characters.

Note: Global settings do not alter previously formatted column settings (example: column A).

CHANGE ROW HEIGHT

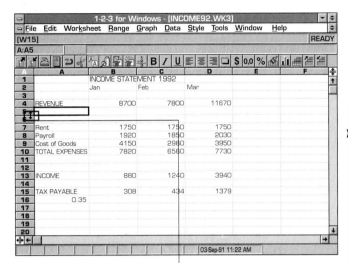

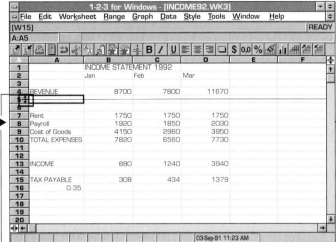

You may want to change the row height to enhance your worksheet.

In the following example, we will change the height of row 5.

1 Move the mouse ⌖ to the bottom edge of a row heading (example: row **5**), and it changes to ✛.

2 Hold down the left button and drag the border to the desired height.

CHANGE ROW HEIGHT

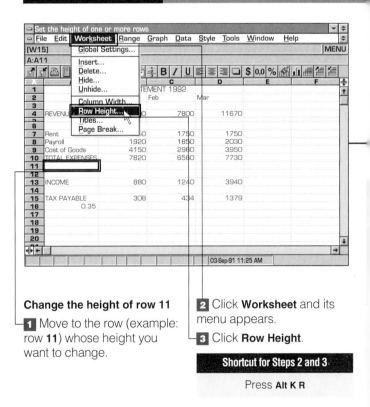

Change the height of row 11

1 Move to the row (example: row **11**) whose height you want to change.

2 Click **Worksheet** and its menu appears.

3 Click **Row Height**.

Shortcut for Steps 2 and 3

Press **Alt K R**

CHANGE
COLUMN WIDTH

**CHANGE
ROW HEIGHT**

INSERT A ROW
OR COLUMN

DELETE A ROW
OR COLUMN

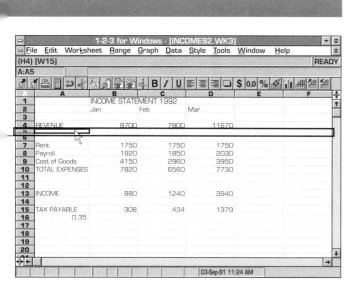

3 Release the button and
the height of row **5** is
changed.

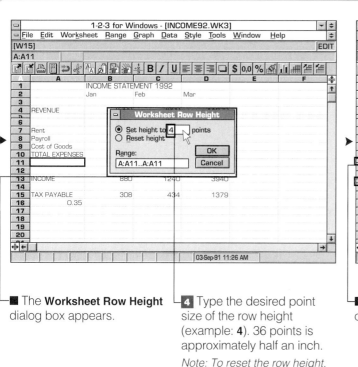

■ The **Worksheet Row Height**
dialog box appears.

4 Type the desired point
size of the row height
(example: **4**). 36 points is
approximately half an inch.

*Note: To reset the row height,
click the circle beside* **Reset
height** *(○ becomes ⊙).*

■ Press **Enter** and the height
of row **11** is changed.

■ The same method can be
used to change the height of
row **14**, or any other row on
the worksheet.

GETTING
STARTED

SMARTICONS

ENTER DATA

SAVE
AND OPEN
WORKSHEETS

MOVE
AND COPY
DATA

ROWS AND
COLUMNS

CHANGE
APPEARANCE
OF DATA

MULTIPLE
WORKSHEET
FILE

CREATE
A GRAPH

PRINT

CREATE A
DATABASE

INSERT A ROW
OR COLUMN

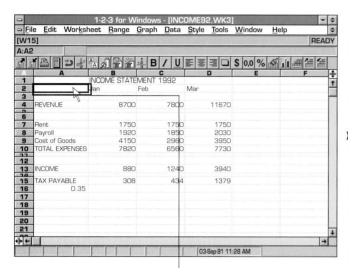

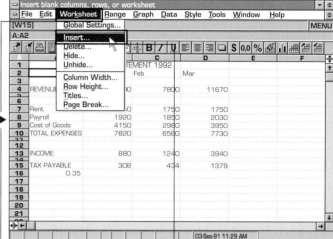

1-2-3 inserts a row above the selected row.

Data in the selected row and below is automatically shifted downward.

1 To insert a row above row **2** click anywhere in row 2 (example: cell **A2**).

*Note: To insert multiple rows (example: 3 rows), click **A2** and drag down to **A4**.*

2 Click **Worksheet** and its menu appears.

3 Click **Insert** and its dialog box appears on the next screen.

Shortcut for Steps 2 and 3

Press **Alt K I**

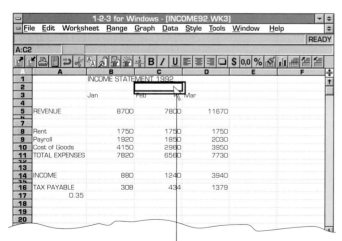

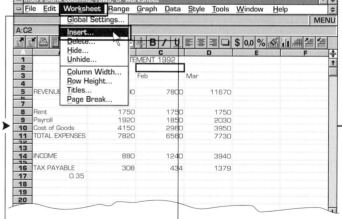

1-2-3 inserts a column to the left of the selected column.

Data in the selected column and to the right is automatically shifted sideways.

1 To insert a column to the left of column **C** click anywhere in column C (example: cell **C2**).

*Note: To insert multiple columns (example: 3 columns) click **C2** and drag across to **E2**.*

2 Click **Worksheet** and its menu appears.

3 Click **Insert** and its dialog box appears on the next screen.

Shortcut for Steps 2 and 3

Press **Alt K I**

CHANGE
COLUMN WIDTH

CHANGE
ROW HEIGHT

**INSERT A ROW
OR COLUMN**

DELETE A ROW
OR COLUMN

GETTING
STARTED

SMARTICONS

ENTER DATA

SAVE
AND OPEN
WORKSHEETS

MOVE
AND COPY
DATA

**ROWS AND
COLUMNS**

CHANGE
APPEARANCE
OF DATA

MULTIPLE
WORKSHEET
FILE

CREATE
A GRAPH

PRINT

CREATE A
DATABASE

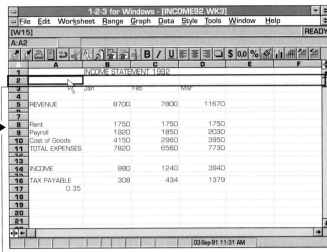

4 Click the **OK** button.

■ A blank row is created.

Note: The number of rows in the worksheet does not change. Data in the worksheet is shifted downward to create the blank row.

*To delete the row, click the **Undo** SmartIcon. This only works immediately after inserting the row.*

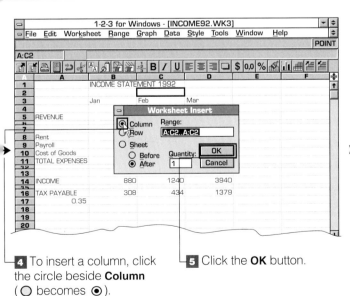

4 To insert a column, click the circle beside **Column** (○ becomes ⊙).

5 Click the **OK** button.

■ A blank column is inserted.

Note: The number of columns in the worksheet does not change. Data in the worksheet is shifted to the right to create the blank column.

*To delete the column, click the **Undo** SmartIcon. This only works immediately after inserting the column.*

DELETE A ROW
OR COLUMN

DELETE A ROW

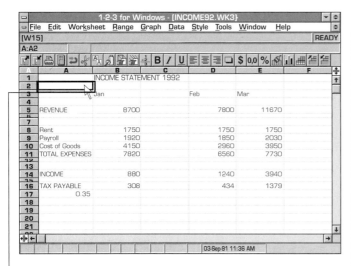

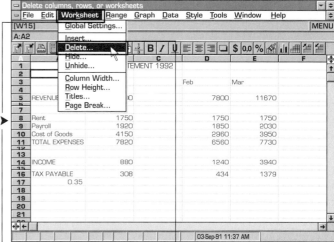

1 Click any cell in the row you want to delete (example: cell **A2** in row **2**).

*Note: To delete multiple rows (example: 3 rows), click **A2** and drag down to **A4**.*

2 Click **Worksheet** and its menu appears.

3 Click **Delete** and its dialog box appears on the next screen.

Shortcut for Steps 2 and 3

Press **Alt K D**

DELETE A COLUMN

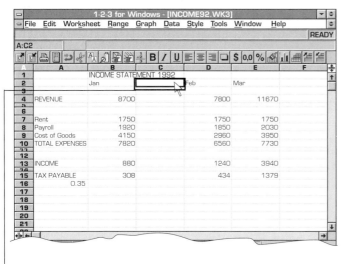

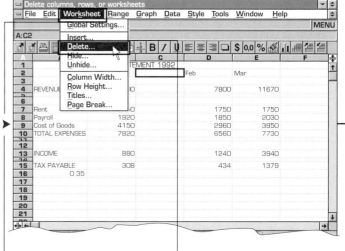

1 Click any cell in the column you want to delete (example: cell **C2** in column **C**).

*Note: To delete multiple columns (example: 3 columns), click **C2** and drag across to **E2**.*

2 Click **Worksheet** and its menu appears.

3 Click **Delete** and its dialog box appears on the next screen.

Shortcut for Steps 2 and 3

Press **Alt K D**

GETTING STARTED

SMARTICONS

ENTER DATA

SAVE AND OPEN WORKSHEETS

MOVE AND COPY DATA

ROWS AND COLUMNS

CHANGE APPEARANCE OF DATA

MULTIPLE WORKSHEET FILE

CREATE A GRAPH

PRINT

CREATE A DATABASE

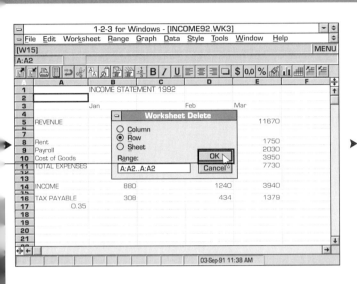

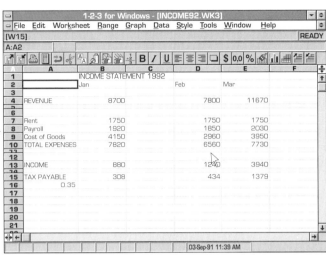

■4 Click the **OK** button.

■ The row is deleted.

*Note: If a formula references cells from a row that is deleted, **ERR** (error) appears.*

*Note: To cancel the deletion, click the **Undo** ↻ SmartIcon. This only works immediately after deleting a row.*

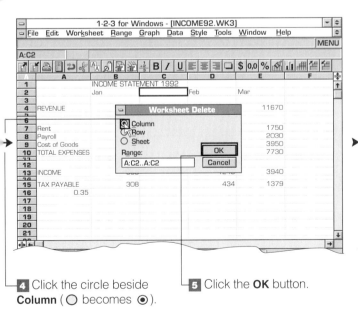

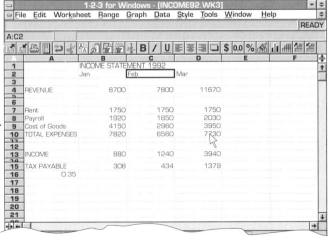

■4 Click the circle beside **Column** (○ becomes ◉).

■5 Click the **OK** button.

■ The column is deleted.

*Note: If a formula references cells from a column that is deleted, **ERR** (error) appears.*

*Note: To cancel the deletion, click the **Undo** ↻ SmartIcon. This only works immediately after deleting a column.*

FORMAT VALUES

FORMAT A RANGE OF VALUES FOR CURRENCY

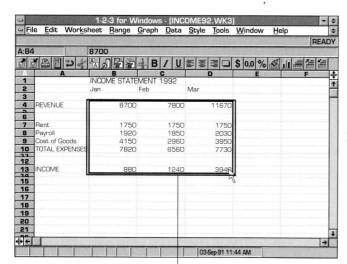

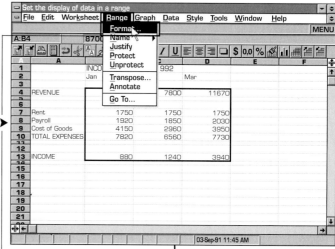

1-2-3 has several built-in number formats to allow you to change the way your data is displayed on the screen.

Note: To simplify the examples in this chapter, the information in rows 15 and 16 was deleted.

1 Select the cells you want to format for currency.

Note: To select a range, refer to page 27.

2 Click **Range** and its menu appears.

3 Click **Format** and its dialog box appears on the next screen.

Shortcut for Steps 2 and 3

Press **Alt R F**.

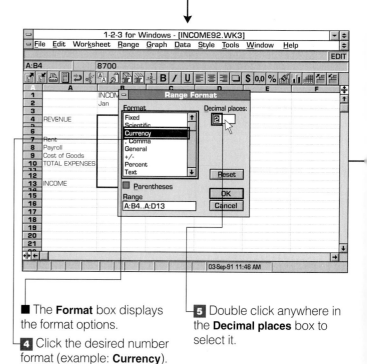

■ The **Format** box displays the format options.

4 Click the desired number format (example: **Currency**).

5 Double click anywhere in the **Decimal places** box to select it.

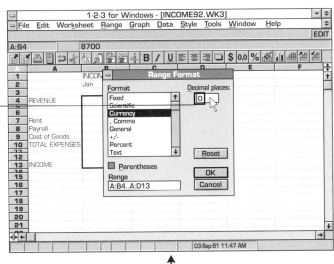

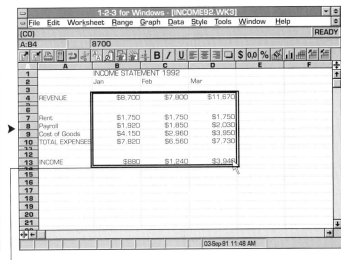

6 Type the number of decimal places (0 to 15) you want 1-2-3 to display (example: type **0**).

*Note: To display the numbers in parentheses, click in the **Parentheses** box (☐ becomes ☒).*

*Click the **Reset** button to change the format to the current global cell format.*

7 Press **Enter** and the selected cells are formatted to display currency.

Note: If the column width is not wide enough to display the new format, asterisks (***) appear in the cell. Refer to page 44 to change the column width.

Format Options	Shown As
Fixed	1000.00
Scientific	1.00E+03
Currency	$1,000.00
Comma	1,000.00
General	1000
Percent	100000.00%

Note: The above table displays values formatted to 2 decimal places.

Format Values Shortcut

1. Select the cells you want to format.
2. Click one of the **Format** SmartIcons:

 Currency (formatted to 2 decimal places)

 Comma (formatted to 0 decimal places)

 Percent (formatted to 2 decimal places)

GETTING STARTED · SMARTICONS · ENTER DATA · SAVE AND OPEN WORKSHEETS · MOVE AND COPY DATA · ROWS AND COLUMNS · CHANGE APPEARANCE OF DATA · MULTIPLE WORKSHEET FILE · CREATE A GRAPH · PRINT · CREATE A DATABASE

◀ 53

CHANGE FONTS

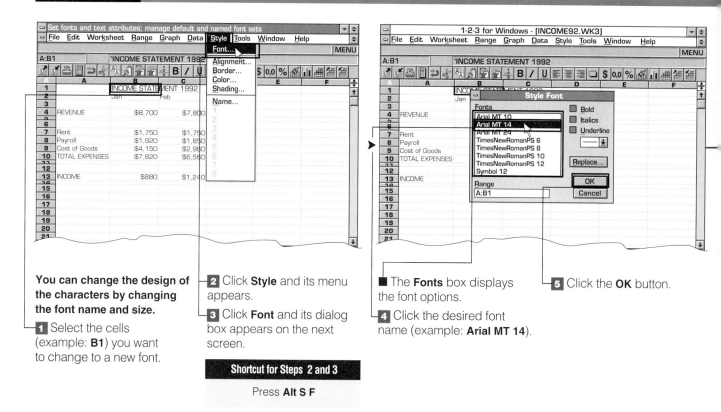

You can change the design of the characters by changing the font name and size.

1 Select the cells (example: **B1**) you want to change to a new font.

2 Click **Style** and its menu appears.

3 Click **Font** and its dialog box appears on the next screen.

Shortcut for Steps 2 and 3

Press **Alt S F**

■ The **Fonts** box displays the font options.

4 Click the desired font name (example: **Arial MT 14**).

5 Click the **OK** button.

ALIGN LABELS

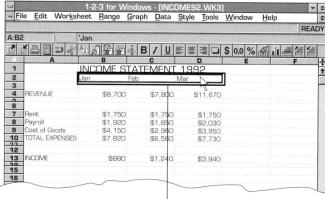

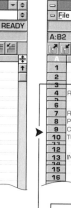

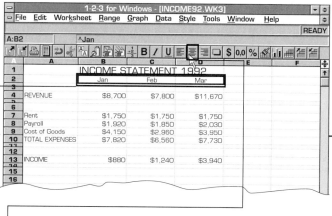

To align a label, you can delete the label prefix and enter a new one. However, the SmartIcons allow you to align a range of labels simultaneously.

Note: You cannot change the alignment of values.

1 Select the cells (example: **B2.D2**) you want to center.

2 Click the **Center** SmartIcon.

■ The selected cells are centered.

Note: Long labels (labels that go beyond the column width) can only be left aligned.

REMEMBER TO SAVE A WORKSHEET USING THIS SMARTICON

Click the **Save** SmartIcon to quickly save your worksheet to the current directory, using the same name.

Note: You should save regularly to prevent losing work due to power failure or hardware malfunctions.

■ The selected range displays the new font style.

Note: 1-2-3 automatically changes the row height to accommodate a font change.

GETTING STARTED

SMARTICONS

ENTER DATA

SAVE AND OPEN WORKSHEETS

MOVE AND COPY DATA

ROWS AND COLUMNS

CHANGE APPEARANCE OF DATA

MULTIPLE WORKSHEET FILE

CREATE A GRAPH

PRINT

CREATE A DATABASE

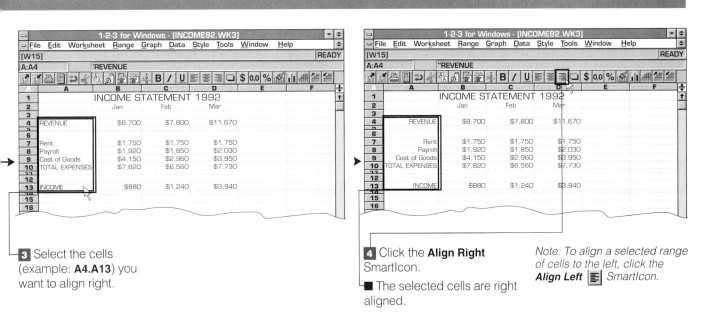

3 Select the cells (example: **A4.A13**) you want to align right.

4 Click the **Align Right** SmartIcon.

■ The selected cells are right aligned.

Note: To align a selected range of cells to the left, click the ***Align Left*** ▤ *SmartIcon.*

BOLD AND ITALICS

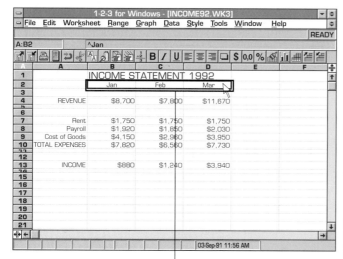

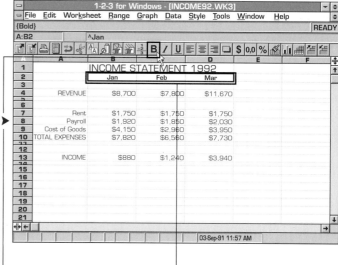

You can quickly change the font style to bold or italics using SmartIcons.

1 Select the range of cells (example: **B2.D2**) you want to make bold.

2 Click the **Bold** SmartIcon.

■ The selected cells are displayed in a bold style.

UNDERLINE

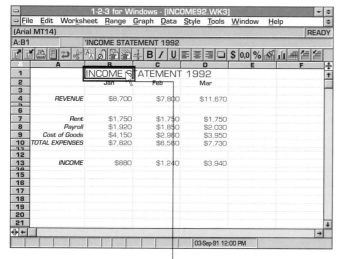

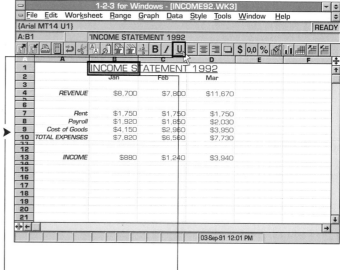

You can underline data quickly and easily by using the Underline SmartIcon.

1 Select the cells (example: **B1**) you want to underline.

2 Click the **Underline** SmartIcon.

■ The data in the selected cells are underlined.

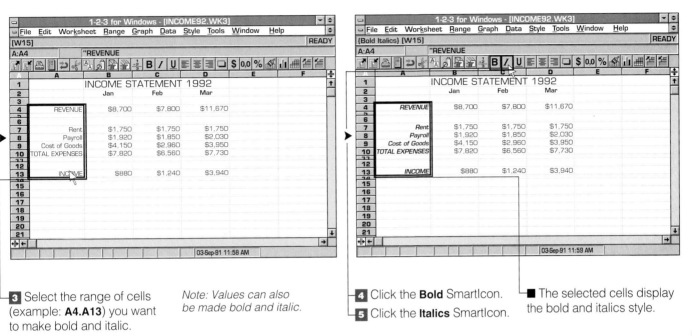

3 Select the range of cells (example: **A4.A13**) you want to make bold and italic.

Note: Values can also be made bold and italic.

4 Click the **Bold** SmartIcon.

5 Click the **Italics** SmartIcon.

■ The selected cells display the bold and italics style.

REMOVE UNDERLINING

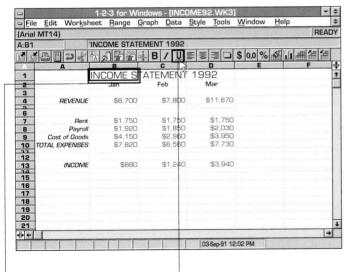

1 Select the cells (example: **B1**) you want to remove the underlining from.

2 Click the **Underline** SmartIcon and the underlining is removed.

To remove bold from a selected range of cells, click the **Bold**  SmartIcon. To remove italics from a selected range of cells, click the **Italics** SmartIcon.

GETTING STARTED

SMARTICONS

ENTER DATA

SAVE AND OPEN WORKSHEETS

MOVE AND COPY DATA

ROWS AND COLUMNS

CHANGE APPEARANCE OF DATA

MULTIPLE WORKSHEET FILE

CREATE A GRAPH

PRINT

CREATE A DATABASE

SHADING

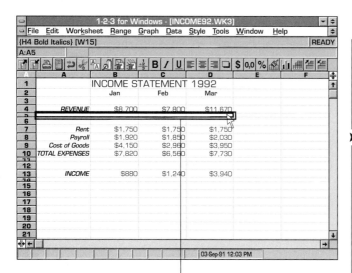
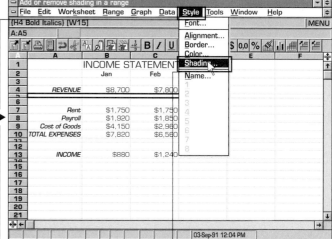

1-2-3 allows you to shade selected areas to enhance your worksheet.

1 Select the range of cells you want to display with shading (example: **A5.D5**).

2 Click **Style** and its menu appears.

3 Click **Shading** and its dialog box appears on the next screen.

Shortcut for Steps 2 and 3

Press **Alt S S**

APPLY CURRENT FORMATS

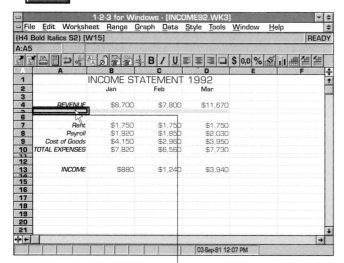
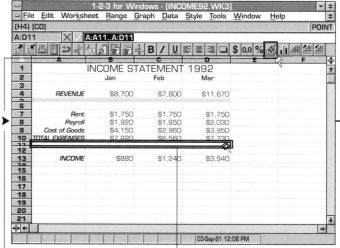

You can apply current formats quickly and consistently to a selected range of cells by using the Apply Current Formats SmartIcon.

1 Select the cell that contains the attributes you want to copy to other cells (example: **A5**).

2 Click the **Apply Current Formats** SmartIcon and the mouse ☞ turns into ✎.

3 Select the range of cells (example: **A11.D11**) you want to apply the current formats to.

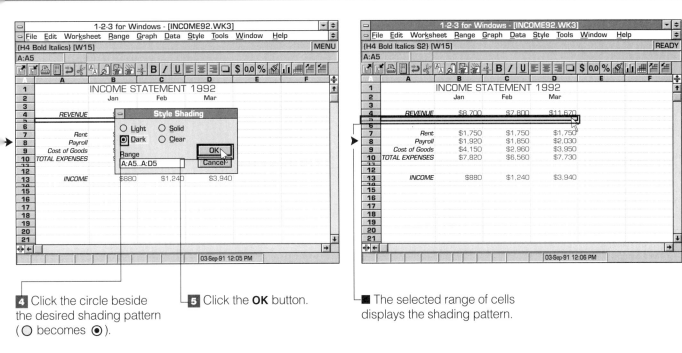

4 Click the circle beside the desired shading pattern (○ becomes ◉).

5 Click the **OK** button.

■ The selected range of cells displays the shading pattern.

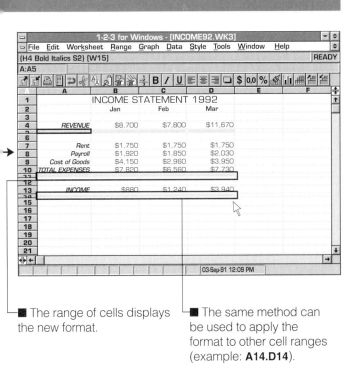

■ The range of cells displays the new format.

■ The same method can be used to apply the format to other cell ranges (example: **A14.D14**).

GETTING STARTED

SMARTICONS

ENTER DATA

SAVE AND OPEN WORKSHEETS

MOVE AND COPY DATA

ROWS AND COLUMNS

CHANGE APPEARANCE OF DATA

MULTIPLE WORKSHEET FILE

CREATE A GRAPH

PRINT

CREATE A DATABASE

ADD COLOR

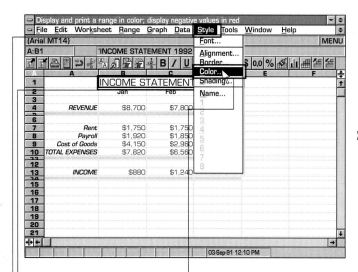

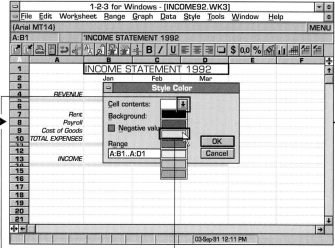

You can display cell ranges in color if you have a color monitor.

1 Select the cells you want to add color to (example: **B1.D1**).

2 Click **Style** and its menu appears.

3 Click **Color** and its dialog box appears on the next screen.

Shortcut for Steps 2 and 3

Press **Alt S C**

4 Click the arrow beside **Cell contents** and the color options appear.

5 Click the desired cell contents color.

REMOVE GRID LINES

Grid lines are the lines on the worksheet that divide rows and columns. These lines can be removed.

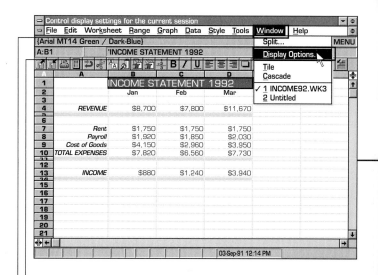

1 Click **Window** and its menu appears.

2 Click **Display Options** and its dialog box appears on the next screen.

Shortcut for Steps 1 and 2

Press **Alt W D**

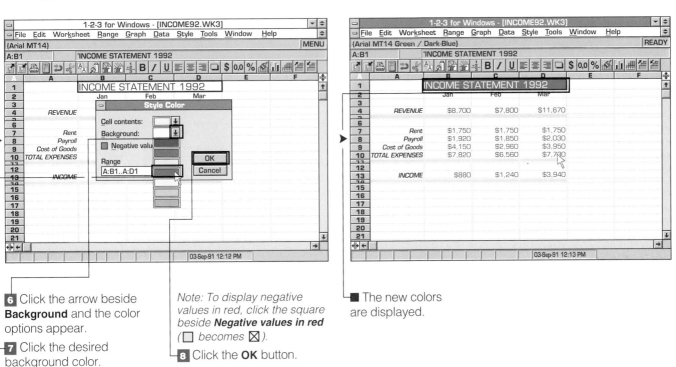

6 Click the arrow beside **Background** and the color options appear.

7 Click the desired background color.

*Note: To display negative values in red, click the square beside **Negative values in red** (☐ becomes ☒).*

8 Click the **OK** button.

■ The new colors are displayed.

GETTING STARTED

SMARTICONS

ENTER DATA

SAVE AND OPEN WORKSHEETS

MOVE AND COPY DATA

ROWS AND COLUMNS

CHANGE APPEARANCE OF DATA

MULTIPLE WORKSHEET FILE

CREATE A GRAPH

PRINT

CREATE A DATABASE

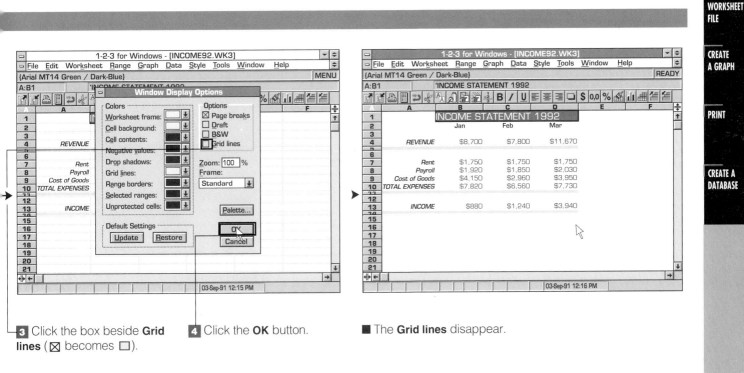

3 Click the box beside **Grid lines** (☒ becomes ☐).

4 Click the **OK** button.

■ The **Grid lines** disappear.

ADD BORDERS

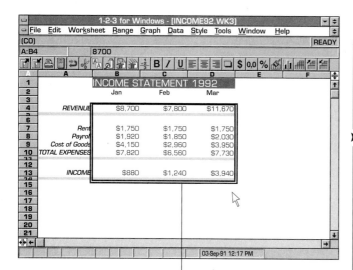

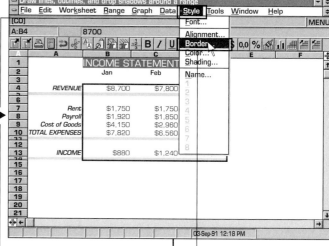

To enhance your worksheet, vertical and horizontal borders can be added.

With 1-2-3 you can add borders to the top, bottom, left, right or all edges of each cell in the selected range.

A drop shadow around the range can also be added.

1 Select the range of cells you want to add borders to.

2 Click **Style** and its menu appears.

3 Click **Border** and its dialog box appears on the next screen.

Shortcut for steps 2 and 3

Press **Alt S B**

4 Click the square beside a desired option (☐ becomes ☒).

5 Click the arrow beside the selected option and the line style options appear.

6 Click the desired line style.

GETTING STARTED

SMARTICONS

ENTER DATA

SAVE AND OPEN WORKSHEETS

MOVE AND COPY DATA

ROWS AND COLUMNS

CHANGE APPEARANCE OF DATA

MULTIPLE WORKSHEET FILE

CREATE A GRAPH

PRINT

CREATE A DATABASE

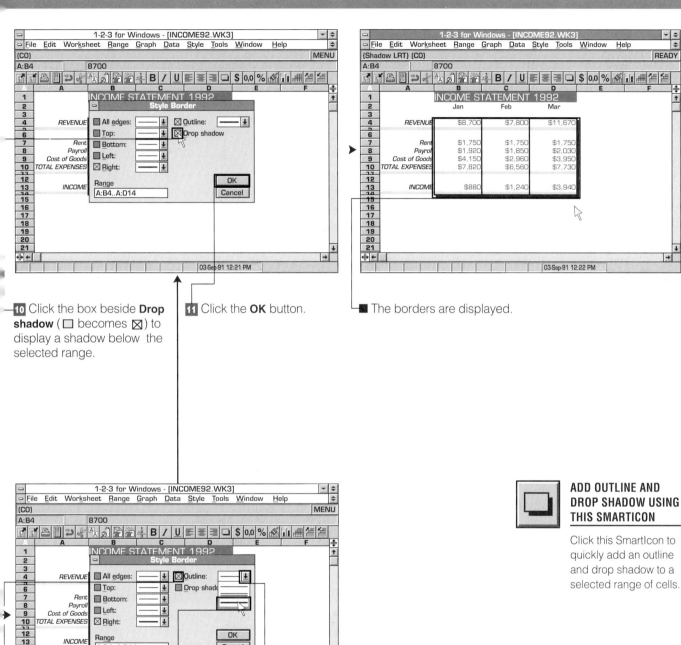

10 Click the box beside **Drop shadow** (□ becomes ⊠) to display a shadow below the selected range.

11 Click the **OK** button.

■ The borders are displayed.

ADD OUTLINE AND DROP SHADOW USING THIS SMARTICON

Click this SmartIcon to quickly add an outline and drop shadow to a selected range of cells.

7 Click the square beside another desired option (□ becomes ⊠).

8 Click the arrow beside the selected option and the line style options appear.

9 Click the desired line style.

CREATE A MULTIPLE WORKSHEET FILE

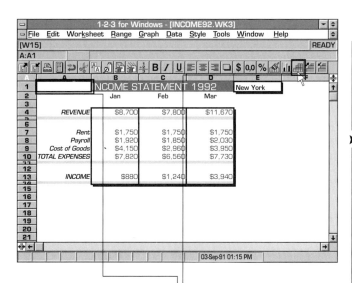

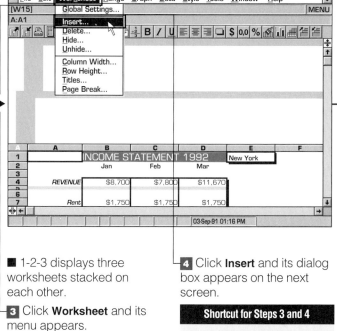

A multiple worksheet file can contain up to 256 separate worksheets.

If you are working with groups of data which are related, but different in structure and format, they can be combined in a multiple worksheet file. Each data group can be placed in a different worksheet (within the same file) and then, structured and formatted using the optimum settings.

Multiple worksheet files also provide an excellent method of consolidating data from several divisions of a company.

In the example that follows, the Income Statements from the New York and Chicago divisions of a company are consolidated.

1 Click cell **A1** to make it the active cell.

2 Click the **Perspective view** SmartIcon.

*Note: **New York** was added to cell **E1** to make this worksheet represent the New York division.*

■ 1-2-3 displays three worksheets stacked on each other.

3 Click **Worksheet** and its menu appears.

4 Click **Insert** and its dialog box appears on the next screen.

Shortcut for Steps 3 and 4

Press **Alt K I**

MOVING BETWEEN WORKSHEETS

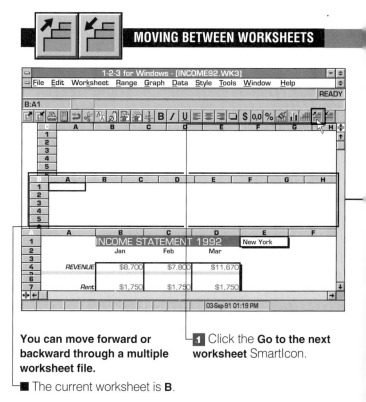

You can move forward or backward through a multiple worksheet file.

■ The current worksheet is **B**.

1 Click the **Go to the next worksheet** SmartIcon.

CREATE
A MULTIPLE
WORKSHEET FILE

MOVING
BETWEEN
WORKSHEETS

TURN ON
GROUP MODE

COPY
BETWEEN
WORKSHEETS

ENTER
FORMULAS

COPY
FORMULAS

GETTING
STARTED

SMARTICONS

ENTER DATA

SAVE
AND OPEN
WORKSHEETS

MOVE
AND COPY
DATA

ROWS AND
COLUMNS

CHANGE
APPEARANCE
OF DATA

MULTIPLE
WORKSHEET
FILE

CREATE
A GRAPH

PRINT

CREATE A
DATABASE

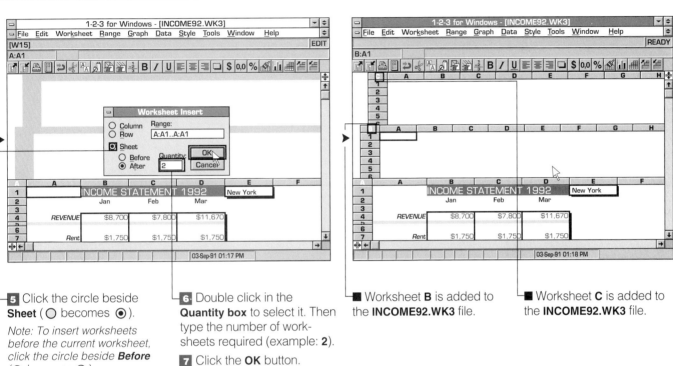

5 Click the circle beside **Sheet** (○ becomes ⦿).

*Note: To insert worksheets before the current worksheet, click the circle beside **Before** (○ becomes ⦿).*

6 Double click in the **Quantity box** to select it. Then type the number of worksheets required (example: **2**).

7 Click the **OK** button.

■ Worksheet **B** is added to the **INCOME92.WK3** file.

■ Worksheet **C** is added to the **INCOME92.WK3** file.

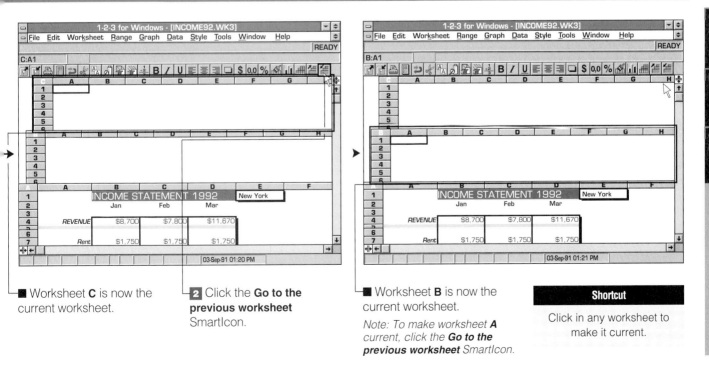

■ Worksheet **C** is now the current worksheet.

2 Click the **Go to the previous worksheet** SmartIcon.

■ Worksheet **B** is now the current worksheet.

*Note: To make worksheet **A** current, click the **Go to the previous worksheet** SmartIcon.*

Shortcut

Click in any worksheet to make it current.

TURN ON GROUP MODE / COPY BETWEEN WORKSHEETS

TURN ON GROUP MODE

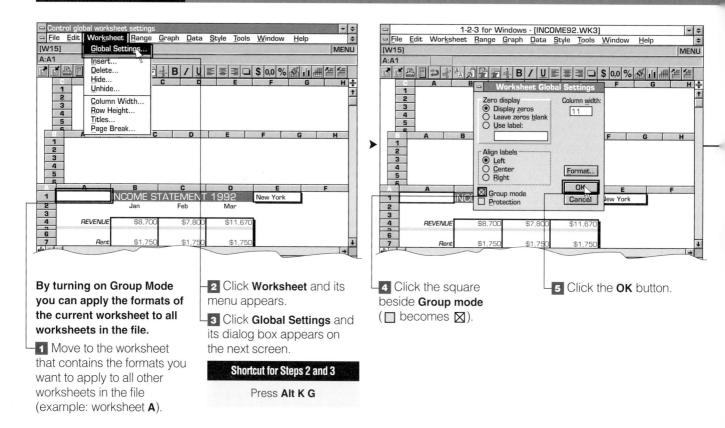

By turning on Group Mode you can apply the formats of the current worksheet to all worksheets in the file.

1 Move to the worksheet that contains the formats you want to apply to all other worksheets in the file (example: worksheet **A**).

2 Click **Worksheet** and its menu appears.

3 Click **Global Settings** and its dialog box appears on the next screen.

Shortcut for Steps 2 and 3

Press **Alt K G**

4 Click the square beside **Group mode** (☐ becomes ☒).

5 Click the **OK** button.

COPY BETWEEN WORKSHEETS

In the following example, part of the New York Income Statement in worksheet A (A:A1.A:E4) is copied to worksheet B (B:A1.B:E4) and C (C:A1.C:E4).

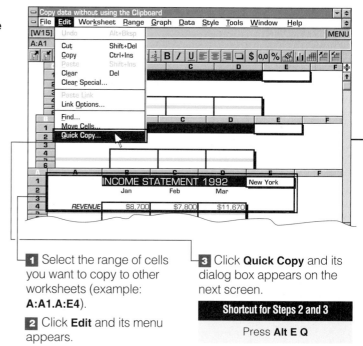

1 Select the range of cells you want to copy to other worksheets (example: **A:A1.A:E4**).

2 Click **Edit** and its menu appears.

3 Click **Quick Copy** and its dialog box appears on the next screen.

Shortcut for Steps 2 and 3

Press **Alt E Q**

CREATE
A MULTIPLE
WORKSHEET FILE

MOVING
BETWEEN
WORKSHEETS

**TURN ON
GROUP MODE**

**COPY
BETWEEN
WORKSHEETS**

ENTER
FORMULAS

COPY
FORMULAS

GETTING
STARTED

SMARTICONS

ENTER DATA

SAVE
AND OPEN
WORKSHEETS

MOVE
AND COPY
DATA

ROWS AND
COLUMNS

CHANGE
APPEARANCE
OF DATA

**MULTIPLE
WORKSHEET
FILE**

CREATE
A GRAPH

PRINT

CREATE A
DATABASE

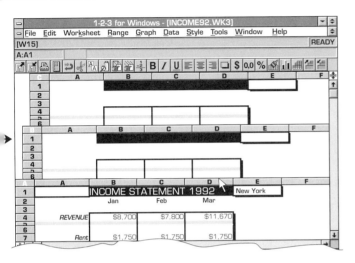

REMEMBER TO SAVE A WORKSHEET USING THIS SMARTICON

Click the **Save** SmartIcon to quickly save your worksheet to the current directory, using the same name.

Note: You should save regularly to prevent losing work due to power failure or hardware malfunctions.

■ All worksheets in the current file display the same global format and styles as worksheet **A**.

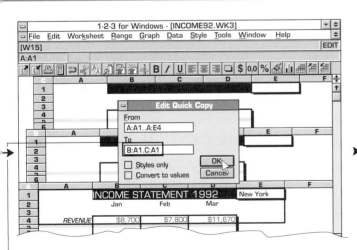

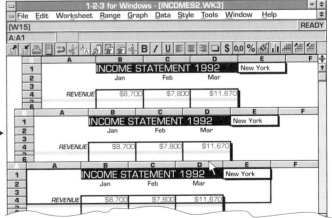

4 Type the range(s) you want to copy the selected data to (example: **B:A1.C:A1**).

Note: The cell address B:A1 tells 1-2-3 to copy the data to worksheet B using cell A1 as

the top left cell address of the new location. The same reasoning applies to the cell address C:A1.

A ▪ (period) separates the worksheet addresses.

5 Press **Enter** and the data selected in range **A:A1.A:E4** of worksheet **A** is copied to worksheets **B** and **C**.

ENTER FORMULAS ACROSS WORKSHEETS

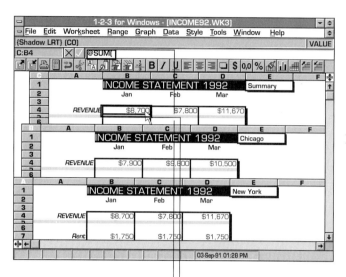

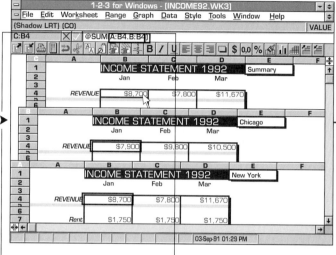

In the following example, the **New York and Chicago Revenue amounts for the month of January will be consolidated on the summary worksheet.**

Note: For this example, the worksheet **B** *REVENUE numbers were changed as follows:* **Jan $7,900**, **Feb $9,800** *and* **Mar $10,500**.
New York *was changed to* **Chicago** *on worksheet* **B** *and to* **Summary** *on worksheet* **C**.

1 Select the cell you want to enter the SUM function into (example: **C:B4**).

2 Type the function and an open parenthesis. For example: **@SUM(**

3 Type the range of cells you want to sum (example: **A:B4.B:B4**).

Note: **A:B4** *defines worksheet* **A**, *cell* **B4**. **B:B4** *defines worksheet* **B**, *cell* **B4**. *The worksheet ranges are separated by a* **.** *(period).*

4 Type **)** (closed parenthesis).

COPY FORMULAS

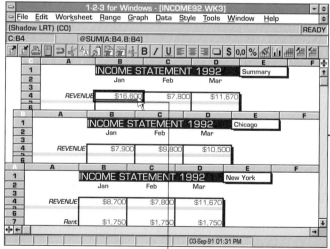

In the following example, the **Revenue formula in cell C:B4 is copied to the Revenue cells for Feb (cell C:C4) and Mar (cell C:D4).**

1 Select the cell (example: **C:B4**) that contains the formula you want to copy to other cells.

CREATE
A MULTIPLE
WORKSHEET FILE

MOVING
BETWEEN
WORKSHEETS

TURN ON
GROUP MODE

COPY
BETWEEN
WORKSHEETS

**ENTER
FORMULAS**

**COPY
FORMULAS**

GETTING
STARTED

SMARTICONS

ENTER DATA

SAVE
AND OPEN
WORKSHEETS

MOVE
AND COPY
DATA

ROWS AND
COLUMNS

CHANGE
APPEARANCE
OF DATA

MULTIPLE
WORKSHEET
FILE

CREATE
A GRAPH

PRINT

CREATE A
DATABASE

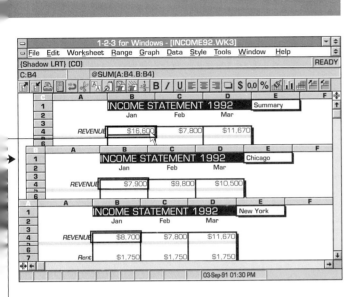

5 Press **Enter** and the sum of **A:B4** plus **B:B4** is displayed.

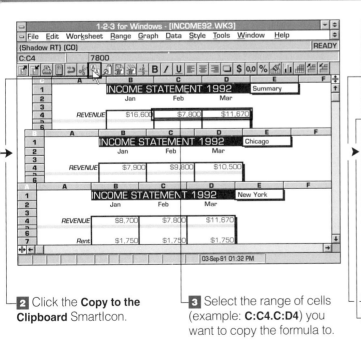

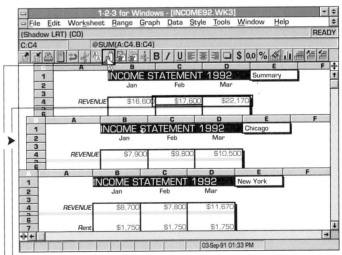

2 Click the **Copy to the Clipboard** SmartIcon.

3 Select the range of cells (example: **C:C4.C:D4**) you want to copy the formula to.

4 Click the **Paste** SmartIcon.

■ The revenues are calculated for the months of Feb and Mar.

*Note: To return to the normal view, click the **Perspective view** SmartIcon. Then click [icon] or [icon] to select the worksheet you want to view in full.*

CREATE A GRAPH

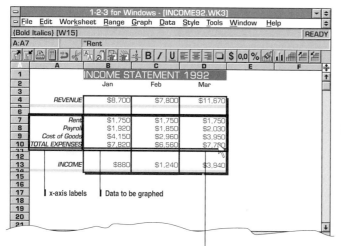

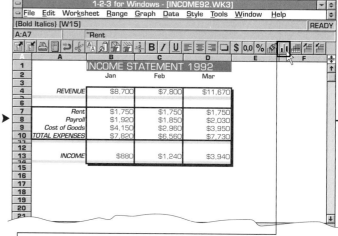

To create a graph you must select a valid data range. The first column in the selected range becomes the x-axis labels. The other columns contain the data to be graphed.

Note: Make sure all your selected cells contain data.

1 Select the range of cells (example: **A7.D10**) you want to graph.

2 Click the **Create Graph** SmartIcon.

CHANGE GRAPH TYPE

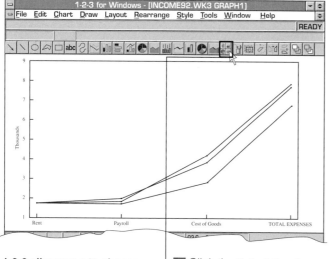

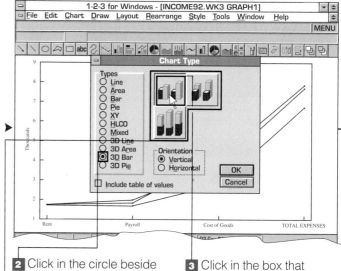

1-2-3 allows you to change the type and style of graph displayed.

1 Click the **Select Graph Type** SmartIcon.

2 Click in the circle beside the desired graph type (example: **3D Bar**).

■ 1-2-3 displays the styles of **3D Bar** graphs available.

3 Click in the box that contains the desired style.

*Note: Click the circle beside **Horizontal** to display the x-axis along the bottom of the graph. Click the square beside **Include table of values** to display data below the graph.*

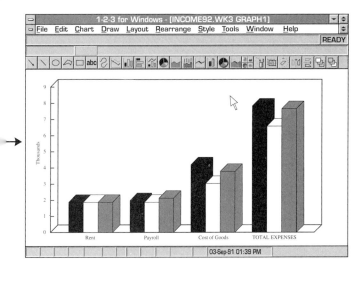

The graph is linked to the
data. This means that if you
later make changes to the
worksheet data, the graph
automatically mirrors those
changes.

■ A graph is created for
the selected data range
(example: **A7.D10**).

*Note: The first graph you
create is named **GRAPH1**.
The next graph created is
named **GRAPH2**. The number
in the graph name increases
by one for each new graph
created.*

CHANGE GRAPH TYPE
USING THE SMARTICONS

Click one of the above SmartIcons to instantly
change the graph type.

4 Press **Enter** and the graph
type is changed.

GETTING
STARTED

SMARTICONS

ENTER DATA

SAVE
AND OPEN
WORKSHEETS

MOVE
AND COPY
DATA

ROWS AND
COLUMNS

CHANGE
APPEARANCE
OF DATA

MULTIPLE
WORKSHEET
FILE

CREATE
A GRAPH

PRINT

CREATE A
DATABASE

ADD A HEADING   ADD A LEGEND

ADD A GRAPH HEADING

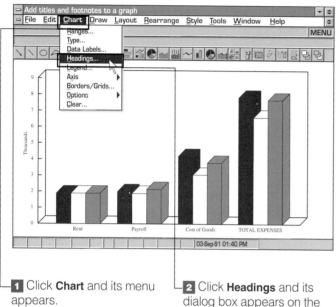

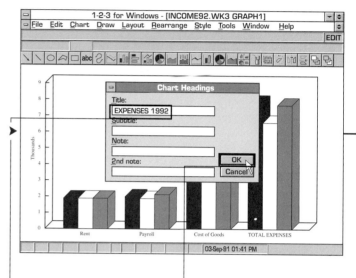

1 Click **Chart** and its menu appears.

2 Click **Headings** and its dialog box appears on the next screen.

> **Shortcut for Steps 1 and 2**
>
> Press **Alt C H**

3 Type the desired heading in the **Title** box (example: **EXPENSES 1992**).

Note: To enter a Subtitle, Note or 2nd note to the graph, click anywhere in the desired box and type a heading.

4 Click the **OK** button.

ADD A LEGEND

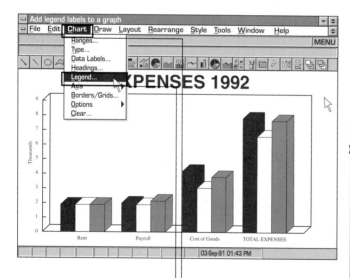

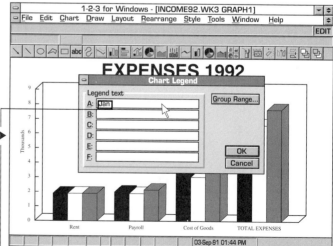

Each data range is distinguished by a different shading pattern. A legend describes these patterns.

1 Click **Chart**.

2 Click **Legend** and its dialog box appears on the next screen.

3 Type the first **Legend text** entry to identify the first data range (example: **Jan**).

72 ▶

CREATE
GRAPH

CHANGE
GRAPH TYPE

ADD
A HEADING

ADD
A LEGEND

ADD GRAPH
TO WORKSHEET

RESIZE
A GRAPH

VIEW GRAPH

ADD TEXT •

DRAW
OBJECTS

MOVE
AN OBJECT

DELETE
AN OBJECT

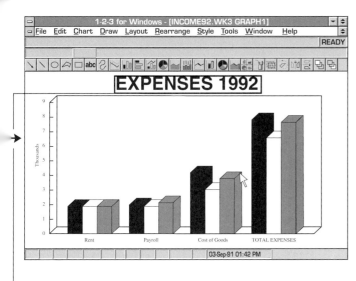

■ The heading is added to
your graph.

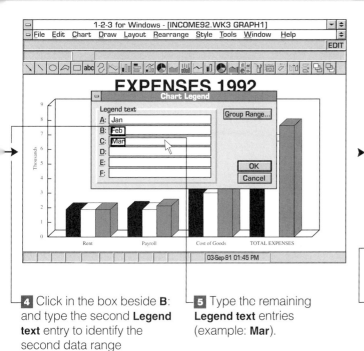

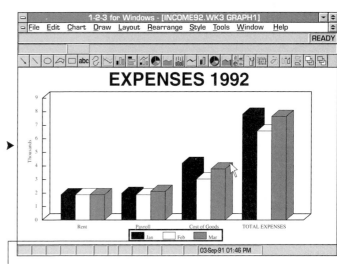

4 Click in the box beside **B:**
and type the second **Legend
text** entry to identify the
second data range
(example: **Feb**).

5 Type the remaining
Legend text entries
(example: **Mar**).

6 Press **Enter** and the
legend is displayed.

GETTING
STARTED

SMARTICONS

ENTER DATA

SAVE
AND OPEN
WORKSHEETS

MOVE
AND COPY
DATA

ROWS AND
COLUMNS

CHANGE
APPEARANCE
OF DATA

MULTIPLE
WORKSHEET
FILE

CREATE
A GRAPH

PRINT

CREATE A
DATABASE

ADD GRAPH TO WORKSHEET

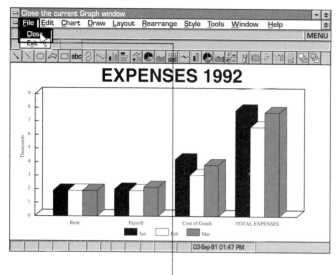

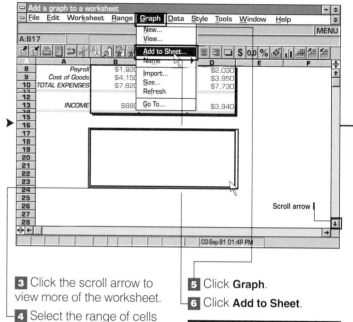

When you add a graph to your worksheet, the graph is sized to fit into the range you specify.

First you must close the graph window to return to your worksheet.

1 Click **File**.

2 Click **Close**.

Shortcut for Steps 1 and 2

Press **Alt F C**

3 Click the scroll arrow to view more of the worksheet.

4 Select the range of cells where you want to place the graph.

5 Click **Graph**.

6 Click **Add to Sheet**.

Shortcut for Steps 5 and 6

Press **Alt G A**

RESIZE A GRAPH

You can resize a graph after adding it to your worksheet.

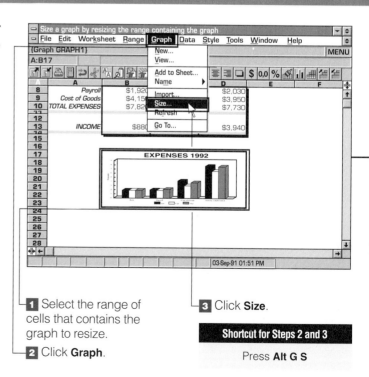

1 Select the range of cells that contains the graph to resize.

2 Click **Graph**.

3 Click **Size**.

Shortcut for Steps 2 and 3

Press **Alt G S**

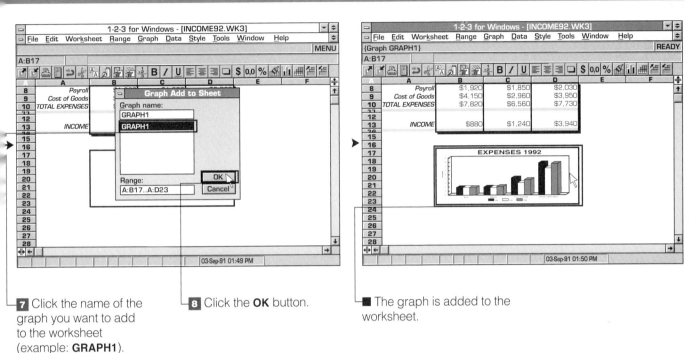

7 Click the name of the graph you want to add to the worksheet (example: **GRAPH1**).

8 Click the **OK** button.

■ The graph is added to the worksheet.

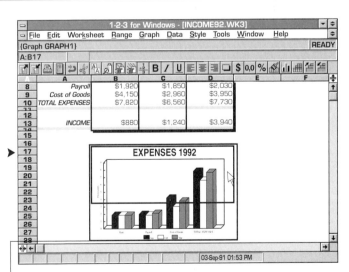

4 Click anywhere in the **Range** box and type a new range of cells. This specifies the new size and/or location of the graph (example: **B17.D28**).

*Note: To specify a range, type the top left cell address followed by a **.** (period) and then the bottom right cell address.*

5 Press **Enter** and the graph is resized on the worksheet.

GETTING STARTED

SMARTICONS

ENTER DATA

SAVE AND OPEN WORKSHEETS

MOVE AND COPY DATA

ROWS AND COLUMNS

CHANGE APPEARANCE OF DATA

MULTIPLE WORKSHEET FILE

CREATE A GRAPH

PRINT

CREATE A DATABASE

VIEW GRAPH

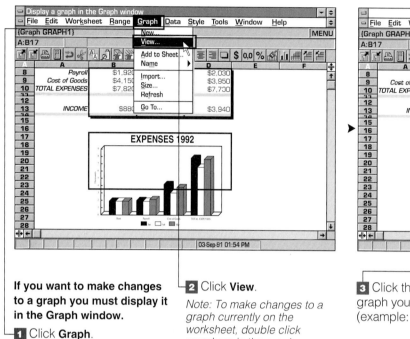

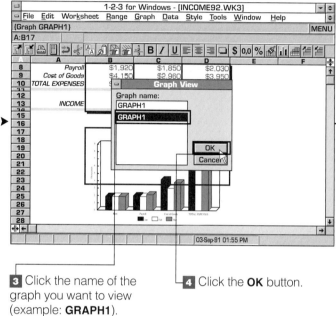

If you want to make changes to a graph you must display it in the Graph window.

1 Click **Graph**.

2 Click **View**.

Note: To make changes to a graph currently on the worksheet, double click anywhere in the graph area.

3 Click the name of the graph you want to view (example: **GRAPH1**).

4 Click the **OK** button.

---

abc ADD TEXT

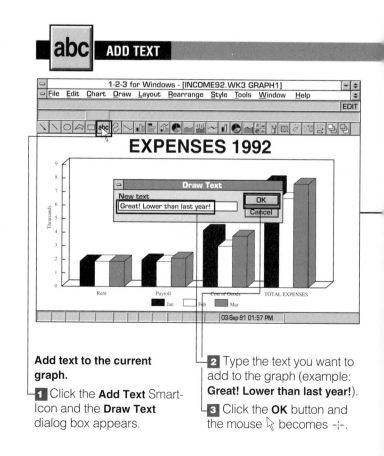

Add text to the current graph.

1 Click the **Add Text** Smart-Icon and the **Draw Text** dialog box appears.

2 Type the text you want to add to the graph (example: **Great! Lower than last year!**).

3 Click the **OK** button and the mouse ↘ becomes -¦-.

EATE
RAPH

CHANGE
GRAPH TYPE

ADD
A HEADING

ADD
A LEGEND

ADD GRAPH
TO WORKSHEET

RESIZE
A GRAPH

VIEW GRAPH **ADD TEXT**

DRAW
OBJECTS

MOVE
AN OBJECT

DELETE
AN OBJECT

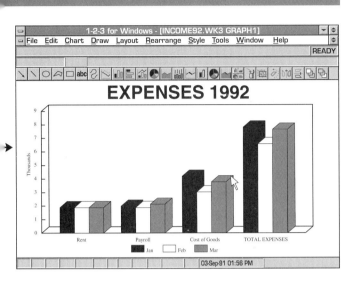

■ The graph is displayed
in the Graph window.
Changes can now be
made to this graph.

GETTING
STARTED

SMARTICONS

ENTER DATA

SAVE
AND OPEN
WORKSHEETS

MOVE
AND COPY
DATA

ROWS AND
COLUMNS

CHANGE
APPEARANCE
OF DATA

MULTIPLE
WORKSHEET
FILE

CREATE
A GRAPH

PRINT

CREATE A
DATABASE

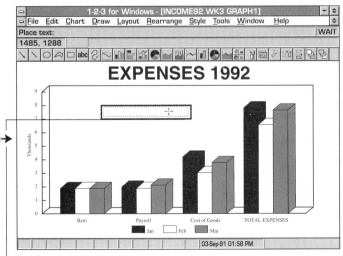

4 Move the mouse to the
position on the screen where
you want the text placed.

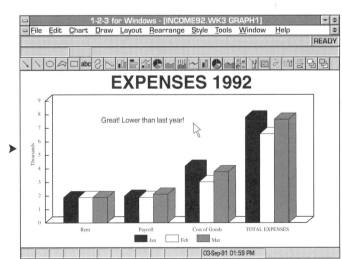

5 Click the mouse button
and the text is placed in the
desired position.

*Note: To deselect the text, click
anywhere outside the text area.*

DRAW SHAPES

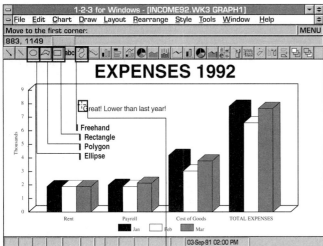

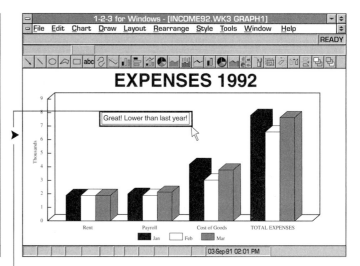

You can add ellipses, circles, polygons, rectangles, squares, and freehand drawings to your graph.

1 Click one of the **Shape** SmartIcons. For example, to draw a rectangle, click the **Rectangle** ▢ SmartIcon. The mouse ⬉ becomes -¦-.

2 Move the cursor to the position where you want to begin drawing the object.

3 Click and hold down the button as you drag the edges of the object to the desired size.

4 Release the button and the object is completed.

Note: When drawing a polygon, anchor each line segment by clicking the mouse button. Complete the polygon by double clicking the mouse button.
*To draw a circle, click the **Ellipse** SmartIcon. Then press and hold down **Shift** during Step 4.*
*To draw a square, click the **Rectangle** SmartIcon. Then press and hold down **Shift** during Step 4.*

MOVE AN OBJECT

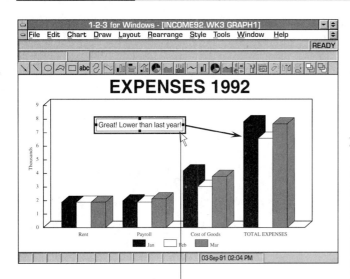

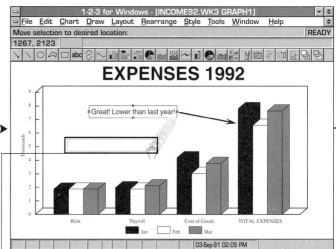

Move an object within the current Graph window.

1 To select an object to be moved, click near one of the object's edges.

2 Click and hold down the mouse button as you drag the object to a new location.

DRAW LINES

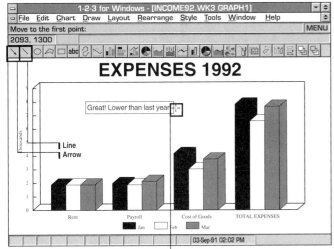

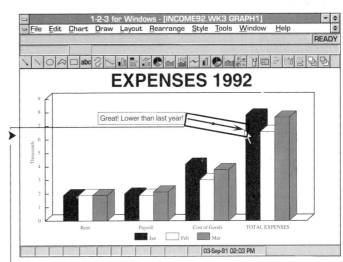

You can add lines and arrows to your graph.

1 Click one of the **Line** SmartIcons. For example, to draw an arrow, click the **Arrow** SmartIcon. The mouse becomes -¦-.

2 Move the cursor to the position where you want to begin drawing the object.

3 Click and hold down the button as you drag the line to the desired length.

4 Double click the mouse button and the line is completed.

DELETE AN OBJECT

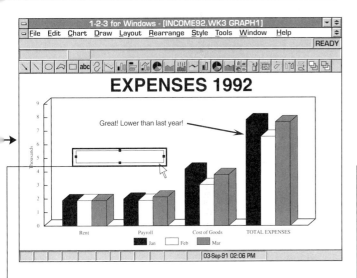

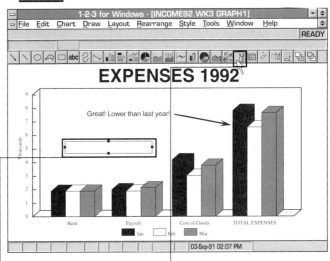

3 Release the mouse button and the object is moved.

Note: To deselect an object, click anywhere outside the object area.

1 To select an object to be permanently deleted, click near one of the object's edges.

2 Click the **Delete** SmartIcon.

*Note: Press **Alt F C** to close the graph window.*

GETTING STARTED

SMARTICONS

ENTER DATA

SAVE AND OPEN WORKSHEETS

MOVE AND COPY DATA

ROWS AND COLUMNS

CHANGE APPEARANCE OF DATA

MULTIPLE WORKSHEET FILE

CREATE A GRAPH

PRINT

CREATE A DATABASE

PRINT
WORKSHEET

PRINT ONE RANGE

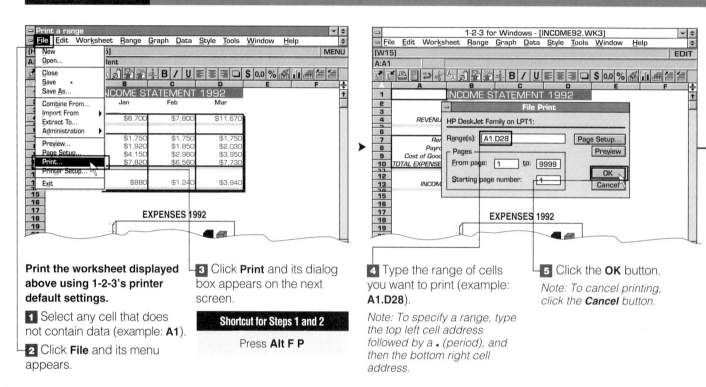

Print the worksheet displayed above using 1-2-3's printer default settings.

1 Select any cell that does not contain data (example: **A1**).

2 Click **File** and its menu appears.

3 Click **Print** and its dialog box appears on the next screen.

Shortcut for Steps 1 and 2

Press **Alt F P**

4 Type the range of cells you want to print (example: **A1.D28**).

Note: To specify a range, type the top left cell address followed by a . (period), and then the bottom right cell address.

5 Click the **OK** button.

*Note: To cancel printing, click the **Cancel** button.*

PRINT MULTIPLE RANGES

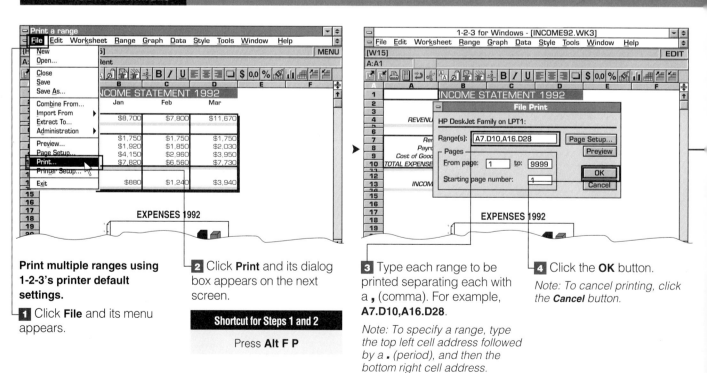

Print multiple ranges using 1-2-3's printer default settings.

1 Click **File** and its menu appears.

2 Click **Print** and its dialog box appears on the next screen.

Shortcut for Steps 1 and 2

Press **Alt F P**

3 Type each range to be printed separating each with a **,** (comma). For example, **A7.D10,A16.D28**.

Note: To specify a range, type the top left cell address followed by a . (period), and then the bottom right cell address.

4 Click the **OK** button.

*Note: To cancel printing, click the **Cancel** button.*

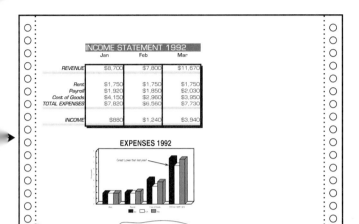

■ 1-2-3 prints the specified range (example: **A1.D28**).

Note: Printing colored areas on your worksheet to a black and white printer may cause problems. The printer recognizes color as shades of gray. Many colors are represented by the same shade of gray and, therefore, cannot be differentiated on a black and white printer.

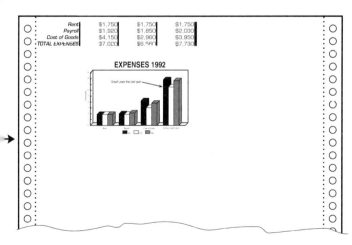

■ 1-2-3 prints the multiple range (example: **A7.D10,A16.D28**).

PRINT USING THE PRINT SMARTICON

Click the **Print** SmartIcon to quickly print a selected range of cells.

GETTING STARTED

SMARTICONS

ENTER DATA

SAVE AND OPEN WORKSHEETS

MOVE AND COPY DATA

ROWS AND COLUMNS

CHANGE APPEARANCE OF DATA

MULTIPLE WORKSHEET FILE

CREATE A GRAPH

PRINT

CREATE A DATABASE

PREVIEW WORKSHEET / CHANGE PAGE SETUP

PREVIEW WORKSHEET BEFORE PRINTING

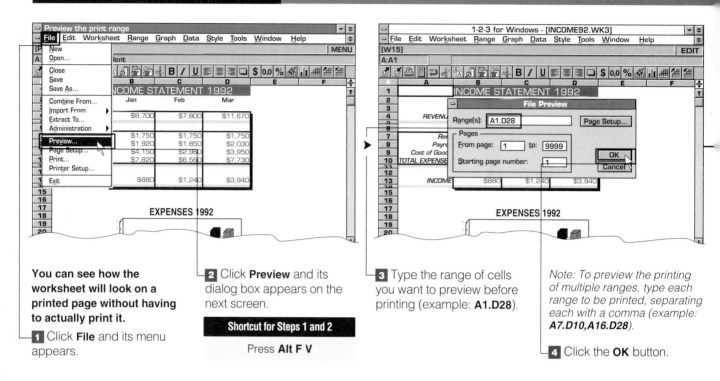

You can see how the worksheet will look on a printed page without having to actually print it.

1 Click **File** and its menu appears.

2 Click **Preview** and its dialog box appears on the next screen.

> **Shortcut for Steps 1 and 2**
>
> Press **Alt F V**

3 Type the range of cells you want to preview before printing (example: **A1.D28**).

Note: To preview the printing of multiple ranges, type each range to be printed, separating each with a comma (example: A7.D10,A16.D28).

4 Click the **OK** button.

ADD HEADER AND GRID LINES TO PRINTED PAGE

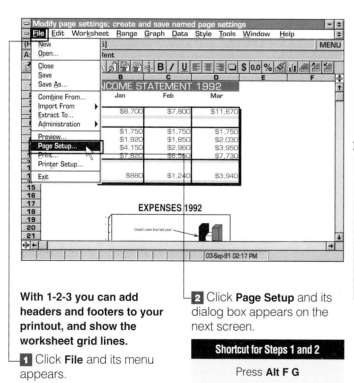

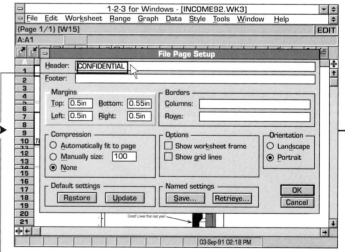

With 1-2-3 you can add headers and footers to your printout, and show the worksheet grid lines.

1 Click **File** and its menu appears.

2 Click **Page Setup** and its dialog box appears on the next screen.

> **Shortcut for Steps 1 and 2**
>
> Press **Alt F G**

3 Click in the **Header** box and type the heading you want to appear just below the top margin of every printed page (example: **CONFIDENTIAL**).

*Note: Use the same method to print a **Footer** just above the bottom margin of every printed page.*

PRINT
WORKSHEET

PREVIEW
WORKSHEET

CHANGE
PAGE SETUP

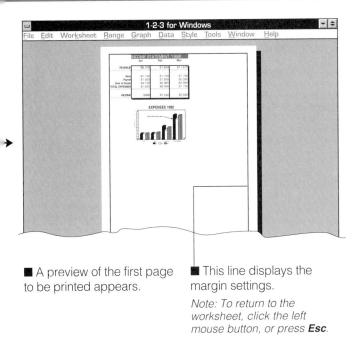

FILE PREVIEW USING THE PREVIEW SMARTICON

Click the **Preview** SmartIcon to quickly preview the worksheet before printing.

GETTING
STARTED

SMARTICONS

ENTER DATA

SAVE
AND OPEN
WORKSHEETS

MOVE
AND COPY
DATA

ROWS AND
COLUMNS

CHANGE
APPEARANCE
OF DATA

MULTIPLE
WORKSHEET
FILE

CREATE
A GRAPH

PRINT

CREATE A
DATABASE

■ A preview of the first page to be printed appears.

■ This line displays the margin settings.

*Note: To return to the worksheet, click the left mouse button, or press **Esc**.*

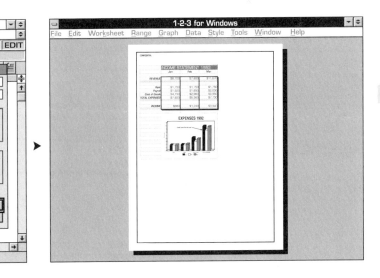

4 Click the square beside **Show grid lines** (□ becomes ⊠).

5 Click the **OK** button.

6 Click the **Preview** SmartIcon and the heading and grid lines are displayed.

*Note: To return to the worksheet, click the left mouse button, or press **Esc**.*

CHANGE
PAGE SETUP

CHANGE MARGINS AND SHOW WORKSHEET FRAME

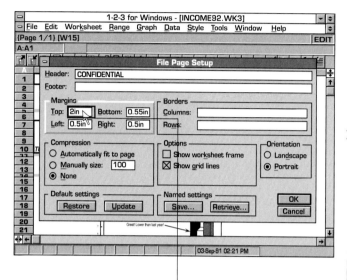

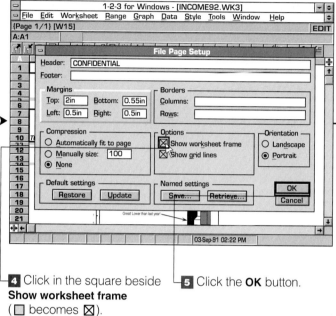

With 1-2-3 you can change the margins of your printout and show the worksheet frame.

1 Press **Alt F G** to access the **File Page Setup** dialog box.

2 Double click in one of the **Margins** boxes (example: **Top**).

3 Type the new margin followed by **in** for inches (example: **2in**).

Note: All margins can be changed in this way.

4 Click in the square beside **Show worksheet frame** (□ becomes ⊠).

5 Click the **OK** button.

SIZE DATA AND CHANGE DEFAULT SETTINGS

With 1-2-3 you can size (make larger or smaller) printed data. The page setup default settings can also be changed.

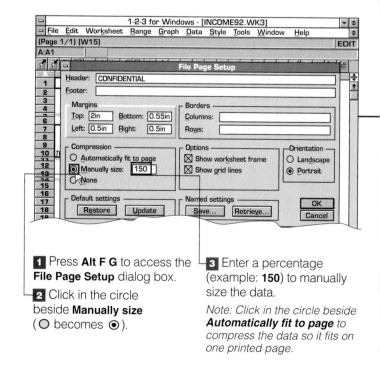

1 Press **Alt F G** to access the **File Page Setup** dialog box.

2 Click in the circle beside **Manually size** (○ becomes ◉).

3 Enter a percentage (example: **150**) to manually size the data.

Note: Click in the circle beside ***Automatically fit to page*** *to compress the data so it fits on one printed page.*

PRINT
WORKSHEET

PREVIEW
WORKSHEET

**CHANGE
PAGE SETUP**

GETTING
STARTED

SMARTICONS

ENTER DATA

SAVE
AND OPEN
WORKSHEETS

MOVE
AND COPY
DATA

ROWS AND
COLUMNS

CHANGE
APPEARANCE
OF DATA

MULTIPLE
WORKSHEET
FILE

CREATE
A GRAPH

PRINT

CREATE A
DATABASE

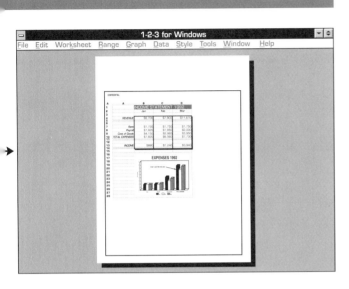

6 Click the **Preview** 🏢 SmartIcon. The new margins and worksheet frame are displayed.

*Note: To return to the worksheet, click the left mouse button, or press **Esc**.*

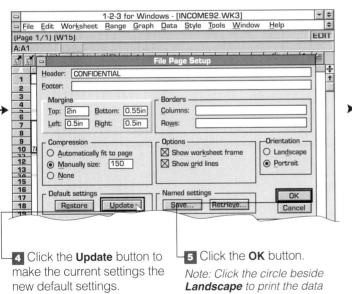

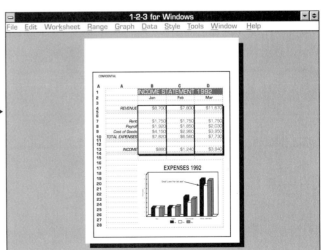

4 Click the **Update** button to make the current settings the new default settings.

*Note: Click the **Restore** button to change the page setup conditions back to the default settings.*

5 Click the **OK** button.

*Note: Click the circle beside **Landscape** to print the data across the width of the paper. (This option is not available on all printers.)*

6 Click the **Preview** 🏢 SmartIcon and the worksheet is sized to 150 per cent.

*Note: To return to the worksheet, click the left mouse button, or press **Esc**.*

CREATE A DATABASE TABLE

CREATE A
DATABASE
TABLE

◆ A database is a collection of related data in rows and columns in a worksheet. It consists of field names (identifies the information in each column) and records (rows of data). Typical databases include library card catalogs, accounts receivable, mailing lists, and telephone lists.

◆ A database can be created using the same skills you have learned creating a worksheet in 1-2-3.

◆ A database is used to organize, manage, sort and retrieve information from large and complex collections of data.

ENTER FIELD NAMES

Rules for Entering Field Names

◆ A field name must be a label. To enter a field name that starts with a number or nonalphabetic character, start it with a label prefix (example: ')

◆ A field name cannot contain the characters , . ; – # or spaces.

◆ A field name cannot look like a cell address (example: F15).

◆ Each field name must be different.

◆ Field names cannot be separated with an empty cell.

ENTER RECORDS

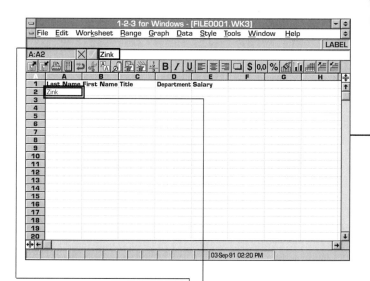

A record is a row filled with information for each field in a database.

1 Select the cell one line below the first field name (example: **A2**).

2 To begin entering your first record, type the data which corresponds to the first field name (example: **Zink**).

CREATE
A DATABASE
TABLE

SORT A
DATABASE

EXTRACT
RECORDS

GETTING
STARTED

SMARTICONS

ENTER DATA

SAVE
AND OPEN
WORKSHEETS

MOVE
AND COPY
DATA

ROWS AND
COLUMNS

CHANGE
APPEARANCE
OF DATA

MULTIPLE
WORKSHEET
FILE

CREATE
A GRAPH

PRINT

CREATE A
DATABASE

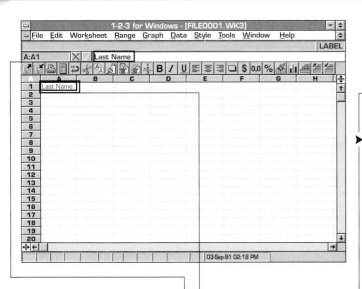

A field name describes the contents of each column.

*Note: Press **Alt F N** to create a new file.*

1 Select the cell you want to enter a field name into (example: **A1**).

2 Type the field name (example: **Last Name**).

3 Press ⏎ to enter the field name and move to the next cell.

4 Type and enter the remaining field names.

Note: To make the field names bold, refer to page 56.

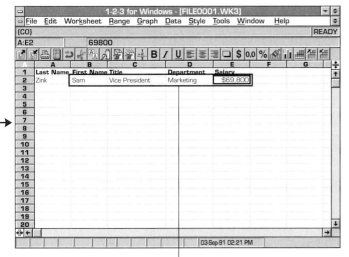

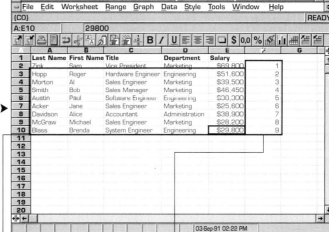

3 Press ⏎ to enter the data and move to the next cell (example: **B2**).

4 Type and enter the remaining data for the first record.

Note: To change column width, refer to page 44.
To format values for currency, refer to page 52.

5 Type and enter the remaining records. Make sure to leave no blank rows between record entries.

6 Type and enter the numbers **1** to **9** in column **F**. This column defines the pre-sorted order of the records.

SORT RECORDS USING ONE OR TWO KEY FIELDS

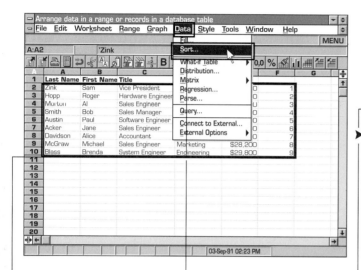

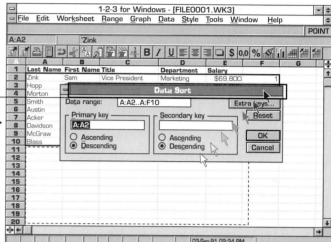

1-2-3 allows you to sort the items in your database using one key field (primary sort) or two key fields (secondary sort). Sorts are performed in either ascending (A-Z, 0-9) or descending (Z-A, 9-0) order.

In the following example, column D (Department) will be used as the primary sort, and column E (Salary) will be used as the secondary sort.

1 Select the range of cells (example: **A2.F10**) you want to sort.

Note: Do not select the field names, otherwise they will be sorted with the data.

2 Click **Data** and its menu appears.

3 Click **Sort** and its dialog box appears on the next screen.

Shortcut for Steps 2 and 3

Press **Alt D S**.

4 Move the **Data Sort** dialog box by dragging its title bar to the desired position.

Note: By moving the dialog box you can view the data while entering the required information.

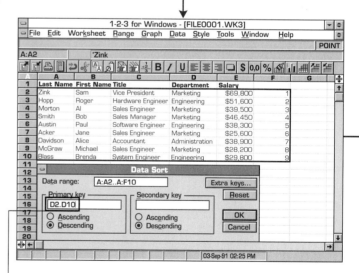

5 Type the range of the column to be used for the primary sort (example: **D2.D10**).

Note: To specify a range, type the top left cell address followed by a ▪ (period), and then the bottom right cell address.

CREATE
A DATABASE
TABLE

**SORT A
DATABASE**

EXTRACT
RECORDS

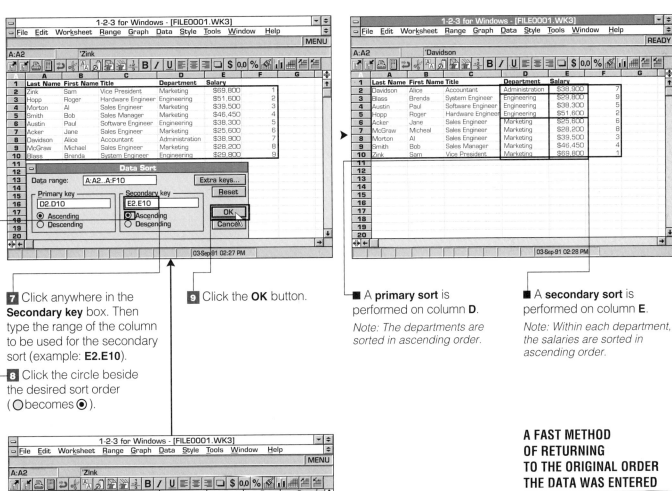

GETTING
STARTED

SMARTICONS

ENTER DATA

SAVE
AND OPEN
WORKSHEETS

MOVE
AND COPY
DATA

ROWS AND
COLUMNS

CHANGE
APPEARANCE
OF DATA

MULTIPLE
WORKSHEET
FILE

CREATE
A GRAPH

PRINT

CREATE A
DATABASE

7 Click anywhere in the **Secondary key** box. Then type the range of the column to be used for the secondary sort (example: **E2.E10**).

8 Click the circle beside the desired sort order (○ becomes ⊙).

9 Click the **OK** button.

■ A **primary sort** is performed on column **D**.

Note: The departments are sorted in ascending order.

■ A **secondary sort** is performed on column **E**.

Note: Within each department, the salaries are sorted in ascending order.

6 Click the circle beside the desired sort order (○ becomes ⊙).

*Note: To only execute a primary sort, click the **OK** button after step **6**.*

Note: Ascending sorts A through Z, and smallest number to largest. Descending sorts Z through A, and largest number to smallest.

A FAST METHOD OF RETURNING TO THE ORIGINAL ORDER THE DATA WAS ENTERED

Select the range of cells previously sorted (example: **A2.F10**).

Execute a primary sort on range **F2.F10**. This returns you to the original order the data was entered.

EXTRACT RECORDS

1-2-3 can easily extract information from a database.

Before extracting data you must define 3 areas: the Input range, Criteria range, and Output range.

The Input range contains the field names and records. The Criteria range contains the criteria that tells 1-2-3 what data to look for. The Output range tells 1-2-3 where to copy the results of the extracted data to.

1 Define the criteria and output ranges by copying the field names to two areas on the worksheet.

Note: To copy ranges, refer to page 40.

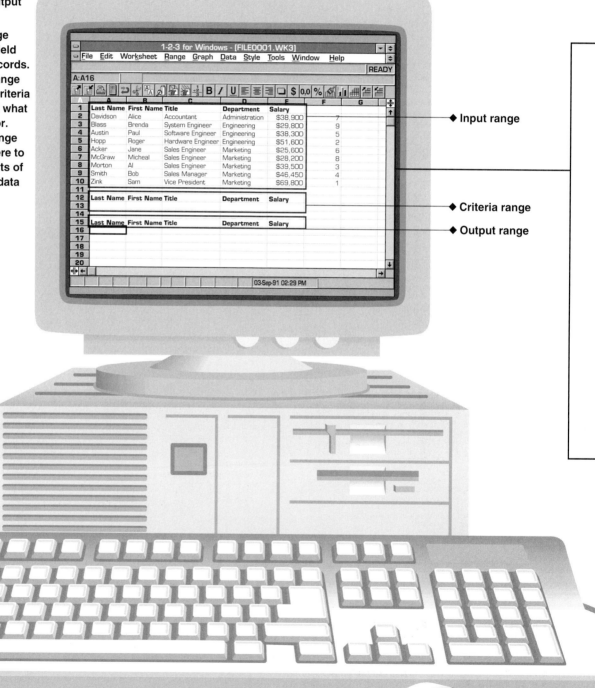

◆ Input range

◆ Criteria range

◆ Output range

The screen shows:

1-2-3 for Windows - [FILE0001.WK3]

File Edit Worksheet Range Graph Data Style Tools Window Help

READY

A:A16

	Last Name	First Name	Title	Department	Salary		
1	Last Name	First Name	Title	Department	Salary		
2	Davidson	Alice	Accountant	Administration	$38,900	7	
3	Blass	Brenda	System Engineer	Engineering	$29,800	9	
4	Austin	Paul	Software Engineer	Engineering	$38,300	5	
5	Hopp	Roger	Hardware Engineer	Engineering	$51,600	2	
6	Acker	Jane	Sales Engineer	Marketing	$25,600	6	
7	McGraw	Micheal	Sales Engineer	Marketing	$28,200	8	
8	Morton	Al	Sales Engineer	Marketing	$39,500	3	
9	Smith	Bob	Sales Manager	Marketing	$46,450	4	
10	Zink	Sam	Vice President	Marketing	$69,800	1	
11							
12	Last Name	First Name	Title	Department	Salary		
13							
14							
15	Last Name	First Name	Title	Department	Salary		
16							
17							
18							
19							
20							

03-Sep-91 02:29 PM

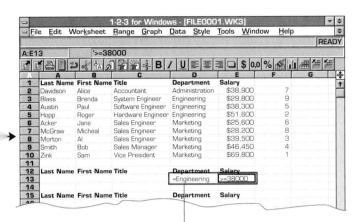

PREFIXES	1-2-3 SEARCHES FOR:
'=	All matching entries
'<>	All entries but that one
'>	All entries appearing after it*
'<	All entries appearing before it*
'>=	All matching entries and those appearing after it*
'<=	All matching entries and those appearing before it*

(sorted alphabetically and numerically)

To enter criteria using prefixes.

Decide what information you want to extract from the database. Then, under the appropriate heading(s), define your criteria.

2 To enter criteria, type a prefix followed by a label or value (example: **'=Engineering** and **'>=38000**). Then press **Enter**.

■ The criteria, in this example, extracts all records in the Engineering department earning $38,000 or more.

Note: When defining criteria, you do not need to format values as they appear in the database. For example, 2100 matches $2,100.

Wildcard Characters

* When you use an * (asterisk) in a label criterion, the * is interpreted to mean any number of characters (example: **'Jo*** matches all entries starting with Jo).

? When you use a **?** (question mark) in a label criterion, the **?** is interpreted to mean any character in that position (example: **'Jo?n** matches Joan and John).

To enter criteria using wildcard characters.

Decide what information you want to extract from the database. Then, under the appropriate heading(s), define your criteria.

2 Enter the criteria (example: **'M***).

■ The criteria, in this example, extracts all records of last names beginning with an M.

GETTING STARTED

SMARTICONS

ENTER DATA

SAVE AND OPEN WORKSHEETS

MOVE AND COPY DATA

ROWS AND COLUMNS

CHANGE APPEARANCE OF DATA

MULTIPLE WORKSHEET FILE

CREATE A GRAPH

PRINT

CREATE A DATABASE

EXTRACT RECORDS

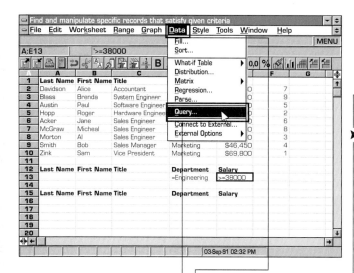

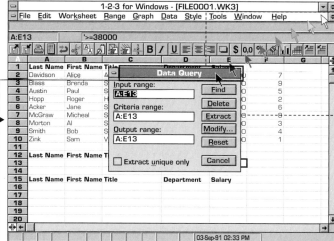

When you extract records from a database you are copying the desired data to a new location.

The data is copied from the input range (the database) to the output range. The criteria tells 1-2-3 what data you are interested in copying.

Once the data is copied to the output range, it can be printed and analyzed.

1 Click **Data** and its menu appears.

2 Click **Query** and its dialog box appears on the next screen.

Shortcut for Steps 1 and 2

Press **Alt D Q**.

3 Move the **Data Query** dialog box by dragging its title bar. This will enable you to view the database more clearly.

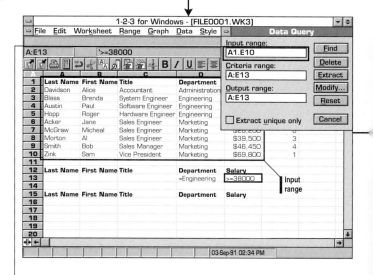

4 Type the **Input range**. Make sure you include the field names in the range (example: **A1.E10**).

Note: To specify a range, type the top left cell address followed by a . (period), and then the bottom right cell address.

CREATE
A DATABASE
TABLE

SORT A
DATABASE

**EXTRACT
RECORDS**

GETTING
STARTED

SMARTICONS

ENTER DATA

SAVE
AND OPEN
WORKSHEETS

MOVE
AND COPY
DATA

ROWS AND
COLUMNS

CHANGE
APPEARANCE
OF DATA

MULTIPLE
WORKSHEET
FILE

CREATE
A GRAPH

PRINT

CREATE A
DATABASE

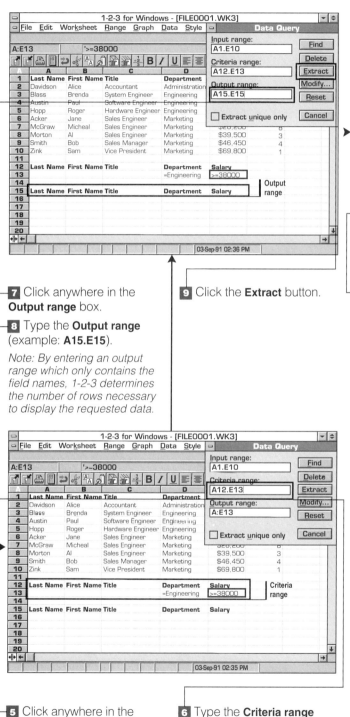

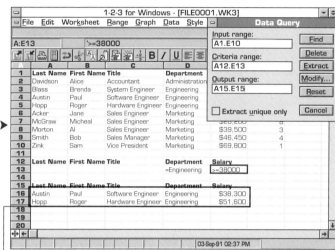

7 Click anywhere in the **Output range** box.

8 Type the **Output range** (example: **A15.E15**).

Note: By entering an output range which only contains the field names, 1-2-3 determines the number of rows necessary to display the requested data.

9 Click the **Extract** button.

■ The requested data satisfying your criteria is extracted.

*Note: Click the **Cancel** button to close the **Data Query** dialog box.*

5 Click anywhere in the **Criteria range** box.

6 Type the **Criteria range** (example: **A12.E13**).

TO SAVE A WORKSHEET

Press **Alt F A** and the **File Save As** dialog box appears. Type a file name (example: **DATA_EMP**). Then press **Enter**.

INDEX